CW00495472

CH
Inside Out

A walk around the ancient walled city

Text, illustrations, maps and publication by

© 1998

Gordon Emery
27 Gladstone Road
CHESTER CH1 4BZ

Printed by

MASONS
Design & Print
River Lane, Saltney
CHESTER CH4 8RH

CREDITS

Thanks to the staff of Chester Record Office, Chester Library and Kall Kwik; Eileen Willshaw (Chester City Council) for the blue plaque copies; Andy Ross for his cormorant; Len Morgan, Nic Fry and Ken Poole for information; Justin for the torch.

Thanks also to those who checked directions and proofread, including Simon Waddington, Roy Wilding, Mike Penney, Tony Bowerman and my family.

Special thanks to Mark W Jones. After reading his 'Snickleways of York', my plans for a hand-written walk guide to Chester was given new impetus. Chester, like York, is based on a Roman fortress. It has gates, streets, medieval lanes, courts and yards, walls, towpaths, 'paths of virtue' through churchyards, riverside walks, ginnels, alleys, passageways and arcades. Therefore it conforms to a city with 'snickleways' according to Mr Jones' definition: "a narrow passage to walk along leading from somewhere to somewhere else".

Unlike York, Chester has a unique system of medieval rows.

If the reader visits York, I can recommend the 'Snickleways' guide.

FOREWORD from Westminster

Chester is an extraordinary city. *Chester Inside Out* will inspire you to return time after time to explore the city's 2000 years of history.

Behind the great architectural treasures, the Roman Walls and Amphitheatre, the unique medieval Rows and the magnificent Cathedral, this book reveals a city full of secrets. You will gain a real insight into the everyday lives of Cestrians throughout the ages – the wares and fares, the inns and taverns, famous faces and Chester Races.

Gordon Emery's earlier books highlighted the beautiful natural landscapes of North Wales. *Chester Inside Out* celebrates the built environment of the city that is the gateway to Wales.

The book will appeal to everyone who loves Chester. Locals will be amazed discover a wealth of nooks and crannies they did not know existed while visitors will be taken on a fascinating tour of Chester's illustrious past.

"Chester pleases my fancy more than any other town I ever saw," declared James Boswell, the biographer of Dr Johnson in 1779.

Read *Chester Inside Out*, explore for yourselves and find out why the legend lives on!

Christine Russell
(Member of Parliament for the City of Chester)

CHESTER

THE LARGEST ROMAN FORTRESS in Great Britain with the largest stone amphitheatre, DEVA may have become Caerleon in Arthur's time and was later known as Legeceaster when Ethelfleda, King Alfred's daughter, rebuilt the walls. Chester was the last English city to hold out against William the Conqueror and, in legend, the refuge of the dying King Harold, mortally wounded at Hastings. Under the rule of its Norman earls its monasteries flourished and its riverside was altered, creating Britain's oldest recorded weir. The earldom held more land in England than any other; one earl even helped to capture the king. During the 14th century the city had the first galleried shopping parades in England with up to six lines of shops in every street, using its unique rows. The Early English stone vaults or cellars are still used. In the 16th century the mayor banned football, as it was becoming too violent, and replaced it with what has become the oldest racecourse in the country. At the same time he introduced compulsory education, three centuries before the rest of England. Another mayor flew in the face of the new English Church by performing the Mystery Plays (now restored) after they were banned. Only the support of the full council saved the mayor from losing his head. In the same century Chester became the first city after London to use a water-powered engine to supply water to its residents. Holding against Parliamentary seige in the Civil War, it was one of the last cities to fall, its citizens resorting to melting down the city's silver to buy supplies, using cathedral roof lead for musket balls, and eating their dogs before surrendering. In 1840 Chester hosted the first British teacher training college, still used today. The first hydro-electric station to power a city was built in 1913 on the site of the famous Dee Mills, using water from the ancient weir. Chester still has the largest unbroken public stretch of city wall in Britain as well as the second most photographed clock in the world. The last Countess of Chester, Diana, Princess of Wales died tragically in 1997. Chester's Earl, His Royal Highness, The Prince of Wales, is heir to the throne.

HOW TO USE THIS GUIDE

walkers

THE WALK is split into four sections. Each one covers a quarter of the city. All the sections start and end at THE CROSS situated at the centre of the city.

Sections are numbered 1 to 4, but you can walk them in any order. Each section can take up to two hours (minimum one hour) depending how often you stop to read the points of interest. There are several museums on section 1, and the cathedral on section 3. Each may take some additional time if you visit them.

There is a map on each double page of the WALK. Route directions to match the maps are in **bold Lettering.** Follow the strip maps from top to bottom.

wanderers

If you don't want to follow the route but just want to wander around the city, you can find the points of interest by reference to the STREET INDEX on page 96 which tells you which page to go to. If you just want to walk around the city walls, follow section 3 until you reach the wall by the belltower, then walk in either direction until you return to the belltower.

features

These are pages without maps which can be read at any time.

armchair readers

Armchair readers don't even have to walk. You can just sit in one of Chester's fine cafés and follow the route with your fingertips, exploring Chester's history as you go.

there and back again

Extensions to the main route are shown in *bold italics* and give you a chance to explore the riverside and canal.

All the blue plaques in the city (except one in Boughton, a mile away) can be found by using this guide. Look for the circle symbol in the text.

A series of green city-shaped plaques can be seen on or near the city walls – a source of more information. *If you still want more information visit the reference section of the city library or the City Record Office in the Town Hall.*

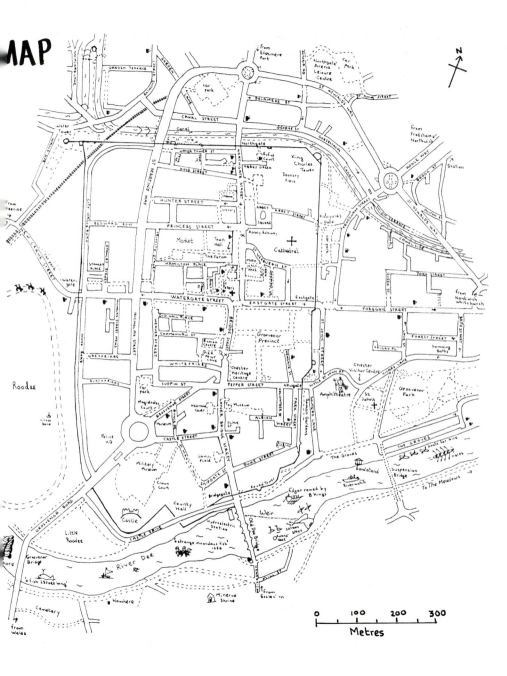

CONTENTS

Four Quarters

of the
CITY OF CHESTER

Based on Hugh
Roberts 'New
Illustrated Plan'
(19th Century)

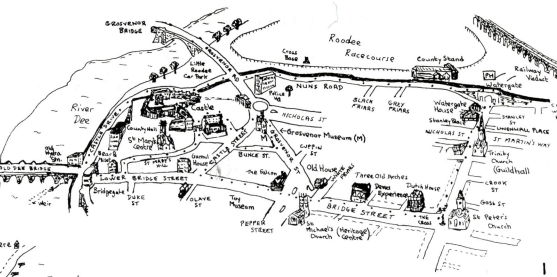

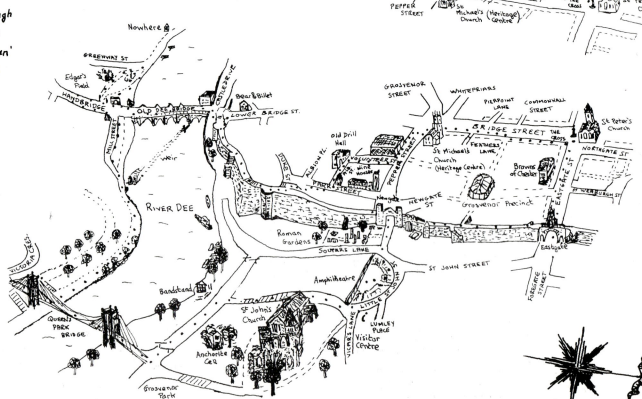

1

2

THE MAPS

FOR the purposes of this walk, the city has been divided into four quarters or sections with the route shown thus:
······

1. Racecourse & Castle: The Roodee, sites of old monasteries, the lower river, the castle and the Grosvenor Museum.

2. River Dee: The upper river, waterfront, bridges and the amphitheatre.

3. Cathedral: The abbey site and the present cathedral, as well as the canal industries.

4. Old Port & Canal: The lower river and old port, with the canal junctions.

Each section, starting from the Cross, has strip maps to help you find your way around. *They are read from the top of each page.* If you can't map read, don't worry. Each section has **route directions** which can be followed with or without reference to the strip maps. The walk starts overleaf.

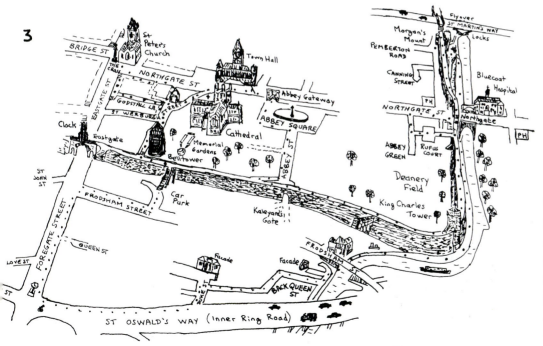

THE WALK

SECTION 1 2·7 Km

Racecourse & Castle

SOUTHWEST QUARTER OF CHESTER

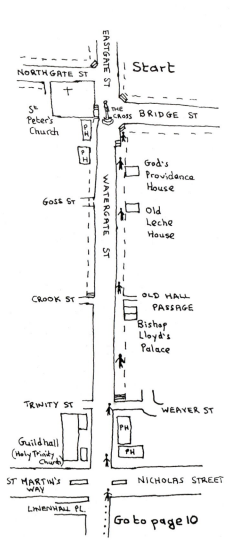

Start

Go to page 10

Ornamental Victorian Sign

THE WALK starts at Chester High Cross. The cross was first recorded in 1377. It was regilded in 1529. In the English Civil War the stone pillar was knocked down after the siege of Chester when the Parliamentarians entered the city in 1646. Three years later Charles I was proclaimed a traitor here.

Sections of the Cross were found hidden under the nearby church steps in 1806 but it was not replaced here until 1975 and even then parts were missing. The base and part of the shaft are in Plas Newydd, Llangollen. Statuettes from the head have never been found.

There was a pillory, used for punishing petty criminals, here in 1356 and a new one set up in 1461 at the cost of a mark.

The Cross is dressed in May

IN 1356 a grant records 'a site in Brugge Street near the stairs leading towards le Corvyserrowe at the end of the Fish Board near the pillory in the corner facing St Peter's Church.' Corvisors were cobblers or shoe-menders and the upper storey or row on Bridge Street West was where they traded. At street level just along Watergate Street was the King's (or Queen's) Fishboard. In 1534, reaffirmed in 1701, all 'Salmon, Mylvell or any other sea Fish' coming into the city had to be sold here. Citizens could buy before 9am, fishmongers had to wait until after while 'foreign fishers' could only 'cut and retail' after 10am. A new 'great bord' was 'set in the Fyshe market' for 3s 8d in 1564.

Ascend the steps onto Watergate Street Row South and continue ahead. At the ninth bay is Old Leche

House. The underlying structure of this building dates from the 14th century and belonged to the descendents of John Leche, surgeon to Edward I. A leche or leech was a physician who probably used leeches to suck the blood of the patient. (Interestingly 'leche' in Spanish is milk. Nowadays medicinal leeches are all the rage in Russia.)

Most of the four-storey timber building may have been erected for Sir John Leche in the 1570s. Inside is an impressive painted chimney front in the galleried hall. There was a hidden priest hole, used to hide Roman Catholic priests in the 17th and early 18th centuries. Behind the grille on the far wall is a 'squint', a spy hole which uses the bars like a one-way mirror. It was used as a watch place when 'illegal' services were held.

The Squint

In 1665 the Linencloth Market was in this row. **Descend the steps at the end of the row and turn onto the street.** Look back up Watergate Street to the large key sign. Below is the oldest locksmith's shop in Britain.

Locksmith's Sign

An invoice from 1595

A note of worke done for the use of the Castill by appointment of Mr James Connstabell of the Castell
the second day of December 1595
of me Edward Powell 1595

Imprimis for meninge A Locke for the castill
gate viijd (8d)
Item for mendinge a Locke for A kitchen door
vjd (6d)
Item for menddinge A hammer for the use of the
keper vjd
Item for mendinge a borket with my own
iron vjd
Item for making a resettes for a pear boultes iiijd
Item for mending a tow pear a shakels xd
Item for making a new key in the queens
bach within the castill iiijd

Continue in front of 'Ye Olde Custom House' Inn. The Custom (& Excire) House is diagonally opposite.

Ye Olde Custom House Inn

Use the pedestrian lights to cross the dual carriageway, Nicholas Street. Numbers 4 to 28 are 18th-century brick terraced houses listed for preservation.

LOOK FOR THE BLUE PLAQUE

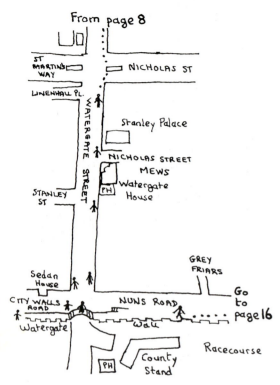

The Stanley Coat of Arms

bears the legend 'Honi soit qui mal y pense' (Shame on him who thinks evil of it). It is the motto of The Most Noble Order of the Garter (1348).

WALK

Stanley Palace

Go downhill, passing Stanley Palace. The building is sometimes open to the public. (You need to ring the bell.) Inside is a panelled room, a 17th century staircase and a Tudor Long Gallery where ladies with long dresses could exercise without getting muddy.

A stained-glass window supports a coat of arms with the legend of the 'eagle and child'. It would seem that Sir Thomas Latham (1327-77), an ancestor to the Stanleys, only had a daughter with his wife. However his mistress, Mary Oscatell, had a son by him. In order to get his wife to adopt the child, the baby was put in an eagle's nest. When Sir Thomas and his wife 'found' the baby in the nest it was suggested that the eagle had stolen the babe. His wife had little option

LOOK FOR THE BLUE PLAQUE

but to look after the poor orphan, who later became Sir Oscatell Latham.

Cross the first side street, Nicholds Street Mews. Watergate House, on the corner, was built in 1820 for the Clerk of the Peace for Cheshire by an architect whose name is synonymous with Chester: Thomas Harrison. *See feature.* The outer curved door in a round porch leads to a large octagonal hall which now has offices of various companies beyond.

Watergate House

Go to page 16

At the traffic lights cross to your right then to your left to reach the Watergate.

Disused Drinking Fountain

The river once ran beneath the city walls. In 1321 tolls taken at the gate included: 'of every horselode of mussells one little dishefull ... of every horselode of great fishe, a quarter of a fishe or the headd or one penny.'

Sedan House

Climb the slope of City Walls Road until you are opposite a protruding porch. It dates to the period when sedan chairs were used as two-manpower taxis for one passenger. The chairmen would enter by one door, let the passenger dismount under cover, then leave by the other. In the 17th and 18th centuries there were as many as fifteen chairmen plying their trade from the Cross. Whilst waiting for fares of sixpence or a shilling, the bearers could while away their time and earn a little extra by whittling vent pegs for beer barrels. In 1820 it was said that, 'the ladies use sedan chairs while the gentlemen usually walk.'

We can guess, then, that the lady who lived here did not want for creature comforts.

Turn sharp left onto the walls and proceed over the Watergate. Follow the flaming torch sign which leads 'To the River Dee,' past the Tattersalls and Paddock racecourse entrance. This is the only racecourse in the country where, if you don't want to place a bet, you can watch the whole course for free — but don't tell everyone or they'll all want to come.

Watergate

Over four hundred years old, Chester Races hosts eleven days of meetings throughout the summer season. *See feature.*

The Tattersalls and Paddock Entrance

Chester Races

HENRY GEE Mayor of Chester in 1540 cancelled the traditional Shrove Tuesday game, where 'one ball of lether caulyd a fout boule to play from thens [the Roodee] to the comen hall', because it was becoming increasingly violent.

He replaced it with 'a bell of sylver to the value of 3s 4d ... to whom shall run best and furthest upon horsebak'.

In 1607 a 'new gallerie' was built on the Roodee at the city's expense. In 1609 an additional race was run with 'Saincte Georges bells and vase of running horses with other pleasant shows invented by Mr Robert Amerye iremonger and sometime sheriff, all these at his coste'.

The sheriffs gave a plate of £13 6s 8d (40 marks) in 1640 for an Easter Tuesday race to replace the traditional 'sheriffs' breakfast'.

Note: there were two sheriffs in the city.

Floods. A cop or embankment was built around the Roodee to keep out the River Dee during 1710 but in 1969 and 1983 races had to be cancelled because of flooding.

IN 1714 the Corporation Plate was added, with 24 guilds donating £25 annually for the race.

A REGISTER of racing colours existed in 1762. Entrance fees for runners during 1777 were 2 guineas for subscribers or 3 guineas for non-subscribers.

Even then, parking charges were in force: John Edmon, Keeper of the Roodee was at liberty to collect 'one day at each Races one Shilling for every Carriage going on the Roodee. And that in Consideration thereof he do not only the Duty of a Keeper of the Roodee but also the Labourers Work which shall be necessary'.

Autumn 1780 saw the Gold Cup race introduced; this was later run in the spring. The year 1802 saw the Earl of Chester's Plate run for 100 guineas.

In 1822 George Brooke, on behalf of 'the Country Gentlemen who attend Chester Races and those who send their horses' petitioned to have 'Races before dinner, after half past two so that the half day's work could be done and those attending the Races have the morning to walk around town to make purchase from the shops'. Country persons might then dine in town'. Needless to say this petition favouring both employers and traders was quickly granted.

The Distance Chair

Clockwise. Horses run anti-clockwise around Chester's 'soup plate' course but the rules of 1707/8 show this was not always the case.

⊥E first paying gate meeting was for the ⌐wly-formed Chester Race Company Ltd ⌐ the spring of 1893. Despite the one ⌐illing minimum charge, crowds of about ⌐ty thousand turned up over three days ⌐t thousands still managed to get in for ⌐thing. Even the Chief Constable of Chester ⌐mitted to opening the gates and letting in ⌐out 200 racegoers for free to stop a ⌐oman being crushed at the turnstile.

⌐e following year a new tradition was ⌐arted. The Tradesmen's Cup which had ⌐egun in 1824, had, under the new company ⌐ecome the Chester Cup: a large silver ⌐unch bowl weighing over 9 kilos was the ⌐rize. Now, further prizes of three ⌐arge Cheshire Cheeses were given ⌐o winner and places.

⌐hort odds. In 1896 Amandier romped ⌐ome for owner Baron de Rothschild ⌐t 25/1 on.

DISASTER struck in 1985 when the County Stand, built in 1899 for £12,500 burnt down. The new stand cost millions and was built in excellent taste to reflect on the character of Britain's oldest racecourse.

Royal Visitors.

Edward, Prince of Wales	1899
George, Prince of Wales	1903
Edward VII	1908
Queen Elizabeth, the Queen Mother	1958
Queen Elizabeth II	1966

War and Unrest. After the English Civil War the Puritan Oliver Cromwell banned the races.
During the war years of 1916-18 and 1940-45 no races were run. The government also stopped racing for the National Strike in 1921 and the army took over the Roodee.

Details of this year's races can be found at the racecourse entrance.

A Day at the Races in 1839

Based on 'Chester Races' engraving.

Feature

ANNUAL RACE ARTICLES
16th March 1707(8)

1. Every horse mare or Gelding that rideth for the plate shall be led out between one and two of the Clock in the afternoon of the same day and shall start at half an hour past two at the usual starting place of the said Roodee leaving all the Poles on the Right hand if any fail therein he is to loose the Race or to run abt the Pole again.

2. Every horse Mare or Gelding that rideth for the plate shall be bridled and sadled and shall Ride with a Rider weighing ten stone fourteen pounds to the stone each Rider to be weighed at the end of every heat and in any want weigh at the end of any heat he shall neither win Plate, Betts or Stakes nor be admitted to run any more for that Plate.

3. Every horse Mare or Gelding that shall be put in shall ride three heats abt all the Poles as aforesaid. Every heat to be three times abt the Roodee and shall not be Rubbed above half an hour be twixt every heat.

4. Such horse mare or Gelding as shall not ride within six score yards of the foremost at the end of any heat should not be admitted to ride anymore and such horse mare or Gelding as shall beat all the Rest the said Distance at the end of any heat shall win the plate without Running any more.

5. No Rider shall start before the word be given for that purpose by one thereunto appointed.

6. No Gentleman or other shall be admitted to put in more than one horse, Mare or Gelding to run for the said plate.

7. Such horse Mare or Gelding as shall run any two heats and keep within distance the other heat shall win the Plate.

8. Every Rider that layeth hold on or strikes any of his ffellow Riders shall neither win Plate, Betts or Stakes.

9. No horse Mare or Gelding shall be admitted to Run for the plate unless he be come into the said city and entred with the clerk of the Pentice six days next before the said Race (the day of their coming in and the day of the Race being included) and continue there from that tyme untill the said Race.

10. If three several horses Mares or Geldings shall win three several Heats then the said several horses Mares or Geldings which did run the said three heats shall ride a fourth heat and that horse Mare or Gelding which shall win the said ffourth heat shall win the plate.

11. If there be not two known able Runners horses entred as aforesaid to Run there shall be no Race, if two horses onely then they shall put in towards the plate fforty shillings apiece, if three horses r they shall put in Thirty Shillings apiece and if more than three horses run there they shall onely put in Twenty Shillings a piece and such person as shall win the said plate shall pay to the clerk of the said race the sum of two shillings eight pence and ten shillings to the poor of the receiving of the said plate.

12. All disputes doubts controversies and differences that shall or may arrise in or concerning these article or this Race shall be decided by the Mayor and Aldermen present or the greatest number thereof.

Galloping Horse *Based on photographs by Eadweard Muybridge*

feature

14

Chester Inns Taverns Pubs & Ale Houses

[OV]ER 500 names have been recorded for [Ch]ester pubs, although only 182 have [exi]sted at one time. Names such as [th]e Sun, Moon, and Angel have gone [to]gether with the Horse and Bags, Dairy [Ma]id, Brewer's Dray, Corkcutters' Arms, [an]d Blackamore's Head which reflect [on] their time period.

[No]wadays you could try a different [pu]b each week of the year. First year [stu]dents try to get round the lot in a [nig]ht (with disastrous results).

[Go]ne too are the breweries such as [Be]nts with their XXX Ale, and the [No]rthgate Brewery which drew its water from deep within the city's bedrock.

LAWS against serving bad beer are recorded from Saxon times. Measures and prices were also strictly controlled from the 16th century. In 1590 the City Assembly ordered that ' ale to be no more than a penny a quart and it to be full.' Even those who served the beer were regulated – women between 14 and 40 years old were banned, from 1540.

Some of the oldest pubs still exist. The Bluebell was just 'The Bell' in 1399 (it is now a restaurant). The Pied Bull was serving beer by 1571 and some say that they can still feel the presence of John Davies who, in 1690, 'casually fell down a pair of stairs leading to the Sellar belonging to the Pide Bull Inn and with a knife in his hand ... and dyed'

The mistake, while painting the name of the Marlbororough Arms in St John Street, has been kept on the new sign.

The widest variety of ales can be found at the George & Dragon, a few hundred metres along Liverpool Road outside the Northgate. The Mill Hotel, along the Chester Canal, and the Ale Taster, beside the River Dee, also have a good range.

Within the walls, real ale can be found at the Shropshire Arms in Northgate Street, the Bear and Billet in Lower Bridge Street and the two 'Firkin' houses: one in Frodsham Street, the other in Watergate Street. Look too for the Fat Cat in Watergate Street. The Falcon and the Boot Inn serve Samuel Smiths : a reasonably priced beer with a hint of oak from the wooden barrels. Outside the walls, the Ship Victory at Gorsestacks and the Union Vaults in Egerton Street cater for individual tastes.

Pub names and ales correct at the time of writing.

feature

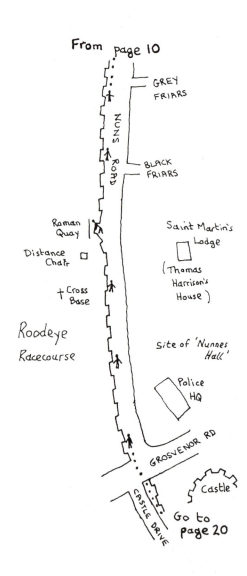

From page 10

GREY FRIARS

NUNS ROAD

BLACK FRIARS

Roman Quay

Distance Chair

Cross Base

Roodeye Racecourse

Saint Martin's Lodge

(Thomas Harrison's House)

Site of 'Nunnes Hall'

Police HQ

GROSVENOR RD

CASTLE DRIVE

Castle

Go to page 20

Continue along the pavement of Nun's Road above the racecourse.

Nun's Road

The roads Grey Friars and Black Friars are on your left. Blackfriars is on the boundary of the former monastery. Dominicans, Black Friars or Friars Preachers, whose rule it was to preach outside the monastery, had come to Chester by 1236. In 1384 Richard II gave the friars leave to grind their corn toll-free at the Dee Mills.

The Friars Minor or Grey Friars also came to Chester. They followed the teachings of St Francis of Assissi. The Grey Friars had their land to the north of Watergate Street where the Linenhall Stables now stand, so the name of the road here is a misnomer. With their belief in poverty it was hard for them to create viable estates. They had arrived in the city by 1238 and in 1245 Henry II let them take

stone from the castle ditch to build their houses and chapel. The Friars allowed fishermen to keep their nets and tackle in the monastic buildings on condition that the fishermen kept their buildings in good repair. By 153? they had a choir, a vestry, a kitchen brewhouse, buttery and poultry house

White Friar (Carmelite)   **Grey Friar** (Franciscan)   **Black Fri** (Dominican)

JUST BEYOND Black Friars, look over the curve of the city wall to the sandstone blocks of the old Roma quay at ground level below (or descend the steps for a closer vie

The river used to run here. Over fiv metres of this ancient harbour wall, which stretched as far as the Waterg

Roman Quay

Cross (Rood) Base

Tower of St Mary's on The Hill

...re now hidden underground. From here ...ooden piers would have stretched out ...to the river.

...ne of the dockhands in Roman times ...as a little careless. About seventeen ...undred years later a pig of lead, ...robably bound for export, was found ...n the mud.

Lead Pig at the Grosvenor Museum

...A SMALL stone pillar beyond the racetrack ...s the base of a cross that gave the ...racecourse its name: Roodee from ...ood (cross) and eye (isle).

FURTHER along the city wall above the Roodee look for a few remaining crenallations used, in medieval times, by archers for firing arrows. When they weren't firing them to defend the city they were practising.

Around 1530 a Chester tutor of Thomas Cromwell's son reported that the son: 'shoot in his Longbow, which trameth and succeedeth so well with him that he seemeth to be thereunto given by nature'.

In 1540 the city Assembly headed by Mayor Henry Gee ordered that on Sunday afternoons: 'boys must shoute and exercise the craft of shoutinge and artillarie' on the Roodee, their parents having to supply bows and arrows.

THE POLICE headquarters and the end of this road are on the site of the Benedictine Nunnery of St Mary, founded in the mid-12th century.

A century after the Dissolution of the monasteries 'Nunnes Hall' became the home of Sir William Brereton, the Cheshire MP who was 'persuaded' to leave the city in the Civil War and ended up taking it a few years later as the commander of the Parliamentary forces.

The strange 'mouldy cheese' architecture of the Police HQ amazingly won a design award when it was built.

17

feature

18

THOMAS HARRISON

MDCCXLIV – MDCCCXXIX

WITHOUT the influence of the architect, Thomas Harrison, Chester would be a very different place. Two entrances to the city are dominated by his works. Approaching from the south, both the Grosvenor Bridge and the Propylaeum (castle entrance) are his designs whereas, from the north, it is the city's Northgate built into the ancient walls. Even the view into Wales has his Jubilee Tower, or the ruin of it, at the highest point of the skyline.

A Yorkshire carpenter's son, he studied in Italy and was impressed by the 'magnificence of the ages'. In Lancaster he designed Skerton Bridge over the Lune, copied by John Rennie for Waterloo and London bridges. The Portico Library and Exchange in Manchester and the Lyceum in Liverpool were built to his plans.

His influence extended to the Embassy at Constantinople where he persuaded Lord Elgin to collect Greek antiquities. The Elgin Marbles are now in the British Museum.

From 1786 to 1810 Harrison planned the Northgate, the Commercial Newsroom, the new County Gaol, Courts, Shire Hall and Propylaeum. During 1820 he built Watergate House and conceived a 'simple but well executed' house for himself: St Martin's Lodge overlooking the Roodee (next to the modern Police HQ).

This 'modest' man, 'shy, reserved and abrupt in his manner' but 'clear and ready in explaining with his pencil' died at the age of 84 in his house opposite the Castle, leaving Chester with an architectural legacy claimed by Pevsner to be 'one of the most powerful monuments of the Greek Revival in the whole of England'.

Thomas
Harrison
1744–1829

Left: The Propylaeum

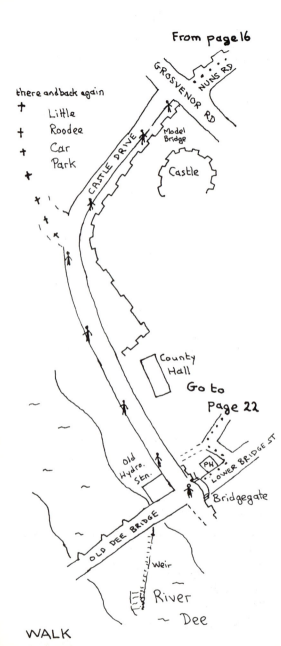

From page 16

GROSVENOR RD
NUNS RD

CASTLE DRIVE

there and back again

✝ Little
✝ Roodee
✝ Car
✝ Park

Model Bridge

Castle

County Hall

Go to Page 22

Old Hydro. Stn.

LOWER BRIDGE ST
PH
Bridgegate

OLD DEE BRIDGE

Weir

River Dee

WALK

Leave Nun's Road using the lights to cross the main road. Keep the city wall to your left and above you as you go down **Castle Drive ahead.** From here is a view of the Grosvenor Bridge to your right. A small model on your left was made by the contractor for the proposed bridge. It was sent piece by piece, by coach to the architect, Thomas Harrison.

Model Bridge

Cross the road and continue downhill.

there and back again

An extension onto the riverside of the Roodee can be made from here except on race days. Go through the Little Roodee Car Park and under the Grosvenor Bridge to reach this open space. Return to Castle Drive to continue the main route.

St. Mary's Without The Walls

AT THE BEND of the road look ahead through the trees to see the spire of St Mary's Without the Walls across the river in Handbridge. Founded in 1885 by the Duke and Duchess of Westminster, this church became the new church for St Mary Parish.

ON YOUR LEFT was the County Gaol built by Thomas Harrison which has now been replaced by County Hall.

Continue to the Old Dee Bridge.

The small arch in the slope up to the Bridgegate on your left marks the top of the former Shipgate, now rebuilt in the Grosvenor Park.

Position of the Shipgate

he road you are on, Castle Drive, was built t a raised level after its removal. For ver a thousand years animals were erded by drovers across the Welsh hills o sell at the markets of this English city, esulting in a thriving leather industry mploying a fifth of the local population uring the 17th century. Skinyards and canneries packed the river bank here, before Castle Drive was built.

Arches in the Old Dee Bridge

Beside the bridge is the former Hydro-electric Power Station. Chester was the first British city to generate hydroelectricity, with three turbines running in 1913, supplying over a third of the city's requirements at a fifth of the cost of other sources.

The Power Station, which is now a water pumping station, is on the site of the Dee Mills built by the Norman Earl Hugh of Chester in the late 11th century. Everyone who wanted their corn ground to flour had to bring their grain to the

mill. The miller then took 1/16th of the flour as payment. The millers were often accused of dishonesty; the animosity between the public and the millers was immortalised in the 'Miller of Dee' written by Bickerstaff in the 18th century: "I care for nobody, no not I, if nobody cares for me."

The mills burnt down several times, the dry dust in the air acting like tinder to a spark, and they were finally knocked down in the early 20th century after being gutted by fire in 1895.

Detail from the Bridgegate

Go through the Bridgegate.
At one time tolls were taken here. In 1321 portions of goods were collected where possible, for example,

'of everie horseloade of oysters or whelkes five And of everie lode nuttes three handfull'.

By 1660 a wagon load of goods cost 8d, a horseload or pack 4d, for every animal sold 1d.

City Benchmark of 1854

AN ORDNANCE Survey benchmark on the road side of the Bridgegate, used for mapping heights was recorded at 31·4 feet above sea level when it was surveyed in the 19th century. Next to it is an even earlier benchmark in the form of an anchor with a solid copper bar inserted into the stone and recorded in the City Treasurer's Accounts of 1854.

Miller of Dee (First verse)
Isaac Bickerstaff 1762

There was a jolly miller once
Lived on the River Dee;
He worked and sang from morn till night,
No soul so blythe as he
And this the burthen of his song
For ever used to be —
"I care for nobody, no not I,
If nobody cares for me."

21

WALK

From page 20

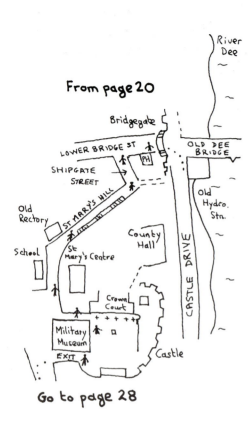

Go to page 28

Cormorants fly up the river to feed

Phalacrocorax carbo

Sketch by Andy Ross

WALK

Bear and Billet

Walk up Lower Bridge Street.

The Bear and Billet LOOK FOR THE BLUE PLAQUE was owned by the sergeants of the Bridgegate and inherited, in 1584, by the Earl of Shrewsbury. It became the Bridgegate Tavern in 1664, after the tolls had been sold to the Corporation, although in 1710 Thomas Williams the innholder, at what was then the Bear Inn, was granted the right to collect tolls on goods over £12.

Look up to the top storey to see the door of an original feature: the granary. Flour and grain was hoisted up here to keep it dry.

Turn first left past 'Ye Olde Edgar' into the cobbled street. The name of the former pub comes from the story of King Edgar the Pacific being rowed up the Dee by eight princes.

Beside the wall is what may have been a mounting block used to help customers get back on their horses when they'd ha a few pints. Steps opposite had a mountir gat

At the next corner of Shipgate Street turn up St Mary's Hill said to be the steepest urban cobbled street in Britain.

St Mary's Hill

22

ON YOUR RIGHT at the top of the hill is the Old Rectory, built in the 18th century and refronted in the 19th. The carriage doors lead into the yard where the stables were situated. Next to the Rectory is St Mary's Hill School which recently celebrated its 150th anniversary.

ST MARY'S CHURCH on your left is now an exhibition centre open to the public. Inside is a richly-decorated roof saved from Basingwerk Abbey, and a brightly-coloured monument to Thomas Gamul, Alice his wife and Francis their son. Gamul was a 16th century 'Recorder' (chairman of the Quarter Sessions) for Chester.

St Mary's has the oldest churchwardens' accounts and parish registers in Cheshire dating from 1536 and 1547 respectively. In 1536 the accounts record:

'It^m Receyued of Robt crosse for A kneling place to his wiff.   xiijd (13d)'

Rushes were spread at Easter and Pentecost. 1537 accounts show:

'It^m pay^d For Rushis Agaynſt Eſt^er. ixd (9d)'

Burial plots had to be bought:

'It^m Receyued of John leche for hiſs wiffs laystall.   xijd (12d)'

and registers written:

'It^m pay^d for a boke to wryte in wedyngs, cryſtenyngs & bereynge   iijd (3d)'

Candles were made:

'Inpmis paid ffor wax for the hole yere.' 24d
'It^m for makyng of the same.'   4d

The registers recorded the cause of death which was sometimes by lawful execution:

'Thomas Laceby a p'ſoner preſt to death bur. in churchyard on the north ſide the ſteeple the 23th day of Aprill.'

Transcriptions can be found in the City Record Office.

Immediately beyond St Mary's Centre turn left into the castle parade ground, now used as a car park.

The Georgian 'Castle' was designed by Thomas Harrison but parts of the medieval castle still exist. To see them, walk alongside the long frontage of the County Hall and Crown Court to the corner gateway. The castle is open to the public daily and has a small exhibition. Look, just inside the gateway, to see the Britannia statue, worn down over the years by soldiers sharpening their bayonets on it.

On the other side of the parade ground is the Propyldeum with an equestrian statue beyond.

After looking around return to the arch where you entered but do not go through it.

Turn along the red tarmac and leave the parade ground by the car exit, passing the Military Museum.

Here, uniforms and battle honours of the Cheshire Regiment are displayed to the public.

LOOK FOR the castle ditch at the road verge. Three 'witches' found guilty at the Michaelmas Assizes in 1656 were hanged, then buried by the ditch at the edge of St Mary's churchyard.

Anne Thornton was found guilty of:

'wickedly divellishly and Feloniously ...exerciſe and practiſe certayne divelliſh and wicked actes and Incantacons called witchcrafts, Incharntments, Charmes and Sorceries in and upon one Daniell Ffinchett'

The three day old baby that Anne had apparently bewitched had 'languiſhed and died' after a few days. Disease, malnutrition or even the wrong blood type were more likely the cause of the baby's demise. The other two 'witches' were convicted of similar 'crimes'.

THE ROUNDABOUT is on the site of Saint Bridget's churchyard and there is still a tomb on it. St Bridget's, one of Chester's nine medieval parish churches, was removed to make way for the new Grosvenor Street.

CHESTER CASTLE

WHETHER a castle existed here in Saxon times is unknown but the first Norman earl, Hugo d'Avranches, built a motte and bailey which would have consisted of a wooden tower and an outer wooden stockade. After 1237, when the last Norman earl died without issue, Chester reverted to the Crown. Henry II ordered the bailey to be replaced by stone and lime in 1245, presumably to strengthen it against Welsh attacks. In 1246, Owen ap Gruffydd escaped from imprisonment in the castle to fight with his brother Llewelyn against the English. Later, Edward I used the castle as a base for his successful campaigns in Wales. The halls of Chester Castle were restyled for the royal personage: Reynold de Grey, the constable, received payment for money spent on 'painting and colouring ten corbels in the King's Great new chamber.'

St Mary de Castro.
The chapel in the 'Agricola Tower' still has the remains of medieval wall paintings.

feature

BETWEEN 1284 and 1291 nearly £1,500 were spent on Chester Castle during the greatest period of castle building in British history.

Heads will roll.
The head of Piers Leigh, a supporter of Richard II, was placed on the castle tower after he was executed by Bolingbroke.

BOLINGBROKE (later Henry IV) took Chester in 1399. He captured Richard II at Flint and held him in the castle overnight on his way to London.

Ball and chain.
In 1397 Thomas le Wodeward, deputy constable of the castle, received new supplies for the gaol:

- 11 iron collars with 2 gross of iron chain
- 2 pairs of iron belts with iron shackles
- 2 pairs of iron handcuffs with 4 iron shackles
- 7 pairs of iron fetters for feet with 3 shackles
- 1 hasp for the stocks

IN the 16th century troops were mustered in Chester to go to Ireland, and after the Civil War the castle was garrisoned by the army.

DANIEL KING in 'The Vale Royal of England' (1651) stated that the

'Castle is a place having priviledge of it self, and hath a Constable... At the first coming in, is the Gate-house, which is a prison for the whole County, having divers Rooms and Lodgings: And hard within the Gate, is a House, which was sometime the Exchequer, but now the Custom-house. Not far from thence in the Base Court is a deep Well, and there-by Stables, and other Houses of Office. On the left hand is a Chappel; and hard by adjoyning thereunto, the goodly fair and large Shire-Hall newly repaired; where all matters of Law touching the County Palatine are heard, and judicially determined: And at the end thereof

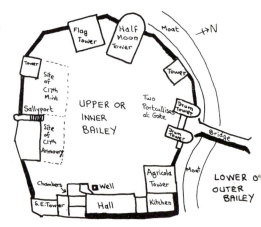

The Castle in the 17th Century

ne brave *New Exchequer*, for the said ounty Palatine: All these are in the Base Court.

hen there is a Draw-Bridge into the inner ward, wherein are divers goodly odgings for the Justices, when they ome: And herein the Constable himself welleth.

he Thieves and Fellons are arraigned in he said Shire-Hall; and, being condemned, are by the Constable of the castle, r his Deputy, delivered to the Sheriffs f the city, a certain distance without he castle-gate, at a Stone called, *The Glovers Stone*: From which place, he said Sheriffs convoy them to the lace of Execution, called *Boughton*.

nother source states that petty criminals were handed over 'att glovers stoune o such officer of the Cittie of Chester, n and from hence to whipp them hrough the Citie'.

Mint condition. Between the years 696 and 1698, silver weighing 46,126 kilos was pressed into coin at the Chester Castle Mint.

THE CASTLE held '16 cartloads of captives' after the Jacobite rising of 1745.

Transported. Many of the rebel Jacobites were sentenced to the colonies. In legend they were taken down a tunnel straight from the cells to the ships in dock so that they never again set foot on English soil.

A LETTER of 1746 shows the problems in the County Gaol:

'There is a very contagious and mortall Distemper in the Castle of which the Gaoler and his wife are dead and Rebells and Debtors in abundance. Since the Gaoler's death the Rebells have attempted to knock the Turnkey's Brains out and have cutt and mangled him desparately (sic)'.

After Thomas Harrison completed the new County Gaol in 1788 conditions were still poor. The Castle Chaplain took pity on the prisoners and put an advert in the Chester Courant 'respecting the misery occasioned by the systems adopted over the previous fortnight, the temperature being from 14°-20° below freezing for five days'. He stated that prisoners, who were kept in solitary cells, had to walk to keep warm and were only allowed to have their 'nuisances removed' once a day.

Needless to say, rather than improve the prisoners' lot, officials chose to discharge the chaplain for interfering with things 'not belonging to his office'.

The medieval 'Agricola Tower'

feature

THE GROSVENOR MUSEUM

STEP INSIDE Chester's compact but interesting museum. Just through the doors are regular temporary displays of history, archaeology and art.

From the hall, decorated with a mosaic including the Chester shield, wander past the stairs into the first room on your left. The life of the Roman fortress of DEVA, its building, its trade and its soldiers are explained in the Newstead Roman History Gallery.

To explore further, use the corridor ahead of the main hall to go into the Graham Webster Roman Stones Gallery. Here, some of the best-preserved Roman tombstones in the world can be found. The stone had been used to fortify the city walls and remained unaffected by the weather until it was discovered in the late 19th century.

Behind the impressive stones is a mural which adds to the atmosphere: 'Hadrian at Deva in 122AD' is by a local artist, Gregory Macmillan.

From Chester Archaeological Journal 1888

Dolphins and a seashell show the deceased in the Blessed Isles of the afterlife. A tripod table, found on all similar stones, may represent stability.

TO SEE Chester in more recent times proceed from the Stones Gallery down the long corridor to the Period Rooms.

The kitchen maid is ironing her apron in front of the warm range in the Victorian Kitchen. Back to modern times for a while as you browse around the shop, then go into the Victorian Parlour. The lady of this house is overseeing her daughter's piano lessons. Upstairs is a Stuart Room, a Georgian Room, a Victorian Nursery and Victorian Bedroom.

UP THE main staircase is the Mayor's Parlour. The Honourable Incorporation was a drinking club that boasted its own spoof 'mayor and officials'.

The Kingsley Natural History Gallery, complete with its own Victorian Naturalist's Study, has varied exhibits such as butterflies and moths, insects in amber, minerals, fossilised fish, sharks' teeth and dinosaur eggs. IT WILL take an hour or so to look around the museum.

Acherontia Atropos

Death's-head Hawk-moth bought for five shillings (25p) in 1820.

feature

LANES

ALTHOUGH THERE are only four 'lanes' within the city walls, this is partly due to the renaming of the streets and house numbering in 1818. Bunce Street was once Bunce Lane, Castle Street was Castle Lane, Shipgate Street was Shipgate or Sheepe Lane.

Other lanes now have different names: White Friars was Custards' Lane, Newgate Street (now partly built on by the Grosvenor Precinct) was Fleshmongers' Lane. Frodsham Street was Cowe Lane, Canning Street was Oxe Lane, King Street was Barn Lane, Princess Street was Parson's Lane, and there is a record of a Bell Lane between the (Blue)Bell and the abbey in the 16th century.

Outside the walls, trade names were prevalent: Leadwork's Lane was Foundry Lane, Steammill Street was Horn Lane, and Union Street was Barkers' Lane (bark for tanning). Souters' Lane is named after the Scotch for cobblers. Love Street was Love Lane.

The remaining four named medieval lanes within the walls are Godstall Lane, Leen Lane, Pierpoint Lane and Feathers Lane. All these four can be seen on the walk.

Other name changes: Black Friars (Lane) = Arderne Lane, Caple Lane led to the Caplegate beside the Old Dee Bridge, Feathers Lane = Dublyn Lane, Linenhall Street = Lower Lane, St Mary's Hill = St Marye Lane, Goss Lane = Gose (Goose) Lane, Weaver Street = Albane Lane, Common hall Street = Lane, St Olave's Street = Lane, St Werburgh's Street = Lane, Cuppins' Street = Lane, Grey Friars (Lane).

Bunce Street formerly Bunce Lane

feature

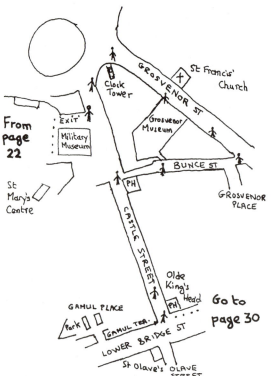

From page 22

Go to page 30

Centurial marker stone at the Grosvenor Museum

Cross the road and go toward the clock tower. Follow the pavement around. Opposite is the Church of St Francis; behind it the only monastery now within the city walls.

Pass the Grosvenor Museum. Open daily, the museum has permanent exhibitions as well as temporary ones. *See feature.*

Turn first right into Bunce Street. Once known as Bunce Lane, the name probably relates to Andreas Bunce who, in about 1260, gave land adjoining Castle Street to Dieulacres Abbey in Staffordshire. This Cistercian monastery, founded in 1214 was named after the exclamation of the abbot on his arrival, "Dieu l'encres" (God prosper it). Originally the monks had resided at Poulton Abbey, a few miles up the River Dee on the Welsh side, founded in 1146 by an officer of Chester's fifth Norman earl, Ranulph II, to pray for the health and safety of his liege lord. The monks, perhaps

Clock Tower

28

fearing for their own safety, packed their ba[gs] and moved across the river after 62 years leaving Poulton Abbey to fall into ruin.

Parish Boundary Marker

ON THE lefthand wall of Bunce Street is a plate marking the boundary of the forme[r] St Michael's Parish. Chester is now one te[a] parish.

At the end of the narrow street turn left. A Sun firemark can be seen up on the wall of the Golden Eag[le]. *See Firefighters feature.* Opposite, a 17th or early 18th century building announ[ces] 'Dominus Illuminatio' (God is light) below the roof. Further on, note the filled-in windows to avoid window tax (1695-18[ ]).

Pass the side of 'Ye Olde King's Head'.   Sign on the wall

COMMIT NO NUISANCE

The 17th-century building is on the site of the earliest recorded stone house in Chester. In 1208, Pete[r] the Clerk, a chief officer of Earl Ranu[lph] III, lived here. Peter was the forerunne[r]

the later mayors: he was allowed to keep [h]is own court and was granted a fishing [b]oat on the Dee above the weir. He [b]ought the house from John Gunde and [A]gnes Outhcarle (names with Scandinavian [o]rigins).

St Olave's Church

ACROSS Lower Bridge Street is the deconsecrated [c]hurch of St Olave. (King Olave [o]f Norway was killed in 1030.) Restored in the 19th century, the building* dates [t]o before the Norman Conquest and reflects the Scandinavian influence in the city. The Scandinavian form of 12 judges is still used in the jury system of Britain and the USA.

*The building before the Conquest may have been wooden.

DOWNHILL is Gamul House, a medieval stone house where King Charles I dined before he fled from Chester. Nowadays, upstairs diners can see some of the features of the building including an ancient door.

UNDER Gamul Terrace a passageway leads to Gamul Place. Inside, to the left is a small hidden park, ideal for a quiet rest away from the bustle of the city.

Gamul Terrace

Turn left up Lower Bridge Street, passing the front of Ye Olde King's Head. LOOK FOR THE BLUE PLAQUE

King Charles on the inn sign

HERITAGE COURT on your left is one of many small courts and yards that used to exist in Chester and Handbridge. Many were demolished in Victorian times because of their overcrowding and unsanitory conditions. A few were saved and this one has been rebuilt as offices.

ACROSS the road is Park House LOOK FOR THE PLAQUE and Tudor House. LOOK FOR THE PLAQUE The latter is said to have been built in 1503 but the date came from a beam which said 1503 and it is reasonably certain that it dates to 1603. Dendrochronological (wood-time) analysis confirms a date within 1592 and 1623. The game of 'I have the oldest building' is played throughout Britain and visitors should treat unconfirmed dates with a pinch of salt.

WALK

From page 28

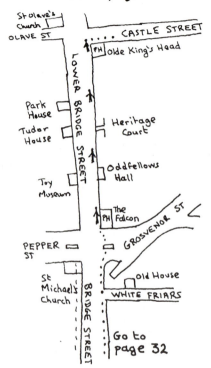

A ROW once ran through the first floor of Tudor House but in 1727 William Bulkeley was granted permission to enclose it on payment of five pounds.

A 'Row' in Lower Bridge Street

A ROW also goes past the Toy Museum opposite. If you like Matchbox cars then you may wish to visit: the museum has the world's largest collection as well as toys from Victorian times onward.

LOOK OUT for Oddfellows Hall on your left as you walk uphill.

The Falcon

AT THE CROSS ROADS is the Falcon This interesting building had an early medieval hall, a later larger hall, and the row in front of it was enclosed when it was the town house of Sir Richard Grosvenor during the Civil War. The City Council could hardly refuse this rich and prominent Royalist when he complained that the house was 'too little to receive his family.'

The Sign of the Falcon

After becoming an alehouse The Falcon went on to become a temperance cocoa house in 1878, then a café. After a short period as industrial premises it fell into disrepair. A restoration scheme saved this historic building and it became a pub once more. Inside, the enclosed shop front still remains as does the wattle-and-daub wall filling on display behind see-through panels. This was made of interweaved branches of hazel or briar, covered with a mix of lime, clay and horse dung

Go to page 32

t the traffic lights cross the road ahead. Look up White Friars, the first road on your left, to see the overhanging timber-framed building known as 'the Old House,' built in 1685.

The Old House

WHITE FRIARS is named after the Carmelite Friars who founded their Chester monastery in 1277. They wore undyed robes or cassocks and took a vow of poverty, chastity and obedience. After the Dissolution of the monasteries, under Henry VIII, the buildings, gardens and orchards of the Black, Grey and White Friars were sold to a John Cokkes of London for £356 6s 10d.

Continue along Bridge Street beside Three Old Arches.

The stone arches reach street level, and behind them is a medieval parallel hall, the largest structure in the Chester Rows.

If you had visited a grocer's shop here in 1613 you might have been given the following bill:

5lb of candied spices	4/-
2lbs of barrel figs	2/-
200 of round wafers	1/6
5lb of Jordayne almonds	7d
200 of walnuts	1/-
five gallons of claret	13/4
5 bottles of strong beer	1/8
2lbs of sugar	4/2
	£1/8/3

All these goods and prices were recorded in the City Treasurer's accounts of 1613. Serving the city as Alderman or Mayor had some advantages.

LOOK ACROSS Bridge Street to the ornate front of a former art gallery. When the gallery was built in the 19th century, the statue of King Charles I was found to be too tall to fit the recess. A drastic solution, and one that did not entail removing any of the poor old king's head again, was needed so the carpenters chopped out a bit of his legs instead.

King Charles I with orb and sceptre is the centrepiece of the Art Gallery front decorated with biblical scenes

WALK

The Falcon
PH
GROSVENOR ST
PEPPER ST
St Michael's Church
Old House
WHITE FRIARS
FEATHERS LANE
Three Old Arches
PIERPOINT LANE
BRIDGE STREET
Dewa Roman Experience
COMMON HALL STREET
Vaults at Nº 12
THE CROSS
EASTGATE ST
WATERGATE ST.
NORTHGATE ST
St Peter's Church
PH PH

Pierpoint Lane is on your left. Alice de Pierpoint was an abbess of St Mary's Nunnery.

IF YOU WISH to see 'On The Air': The Broadcasting Museum, open daily, go up the steps beside the bridge. 'The Dewa Roman Centre', an exhibition of Roman Chester (DEVA) and archaeological digs, is at the end of Pierpoint Lane. Return to Bridge Street to continue.

ABOVE YOU, as mentioned earlier, the row was once Corvisors' Row as far as the Cross. This section was later known as Flax Row.

Pass Commonhall Street on your left. The street once led to the 15th-century 'Comen Hall' or public hall where all merch had to take their imported goods to sell

THE Row above, including the 'Dutch House(s was referred to, in 1860, as Scotch Row.

SOME of the oldest shops recorded in Chester during the 13th century were 'undecim seldas quae vocantur seldae sutorum in Bruggestrete' (eleven stalls called the shoemakers' shops in Bridgestreet). These stalls probably leant against the building at street level.

Return to the High Cross.

In the sixth shop from the Cross (Bookland) is a crypt, found under rubbish in 1839. It probably dates from the late 13th century and is the second oldest in the city. The oldest is said to be at 11 Watergate Street.

WALK

George Cuitt's engraving of 1809 shows The Dutch House. 'House in Bridge Street as it appeared in 1808'.

WALK

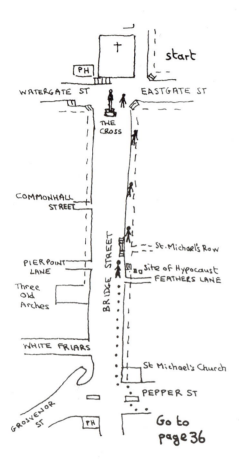

Map labels:
- WATERGATE ST
- EASTGATE ST
- start
- PH
- THE CROSS
- COMMONHALL STREET
- BRIDGE STREET
- St. Michael's Row
- PIERPOINT LANE
- Site of Hypocaust FEATHERS LANE
- Three Old Arches
- WHITE FRIARS
- St Michael's Church
- PEPPER ST
- GROSVENOR ST
- PH
- Go to page 36

THE WALK

SECTION 2

2·7 Km

River Dee

SOUTHEAST QUARTER OF CHESTER

AS BEFORE, this section of the walk starts at Chester High Cross, in front of St Peter's Church. The present church building is mainly from the 15th century with a 19th-century tower. The south wall was rebuilt by Thomas Harrison after the demolition of a two-storey timber-framed building, called the Pentice, was demolished in 1806.

Randle Holmes' sketch of the Pentice also shows the Cross base after the Civil War.

The Pentice, first recorded in 1288, partially blocked this street and, at one time, part of Northgate Street as well. Inside was the council and mayor's offices. The city courts were often held here: the Pentice Court, where the sheriffs dealt with covenants, debt and trespass; and the Portmote Court, presided over by the Mayor for more serious misdemeanors.

Shops below were known as Cookes' Row or Pentice Row. In the 18th century the building was altered to allow access to Northgate Street.

Steps to Bridge Street Row East and Eastgate Street Row South

WALK

LOOK up at the black and white building (of 1888) on the corner of Bridge Street and Eastgate Street to see the city arms and Latin motto granted in 1580: Antiqui Colant Antiquum Dierum (Let the ancients honour the Ancient of Days) Look out for the city arms again on the walk: they appear in ten other places on this section. *

There are still mercers (tailors) on Bridge Street Row East

Go up the steps and walk along Bridge Street Row East. Once known

* The city arms appear on street signs, Grosvenor Precinct stained glass, the Newgate, Queen's Park Bridge, public conveniences, the Eastgate, the Midland Bank, Browns and a shop opposite, and the city bus tour.

as Mercer's Row, it was packed with cloth merchants and tailors.

GEORGE LOWE, the silversmith, had a shop in the Pentice Row before it was demolished. In 1803 he asked the council for permission to take a shop in Bridge Street Row. Lowes have been here ever since.

Halfway along the row is the Edwardian shopping arcade, Saint

Saint Michael's Row
An Edwardian arcade

Michael's Row, to your left. The

blue plaque intended for this arcade was never installed, and thus becomes the only one quoted in this text. It would have read: 'This shopping arcade was built for the second Duke of Westminster by the Chester Architect W T Lockwood in 1910. The original baroque facade was much criticised and in 1911 the white tile frontage was replaced with the present timber framing'.

Take the steps down to street level here and continue along

Bridge Street. Just two shops past the next set of steps is a small shop with an interesting basement, open to the public on request. In it are the remains of a 'hypocaust' set under the 'sudatorium' or sweating room of the once massive Roman baths.

Hypocaust pillars support ventilating floor tiles

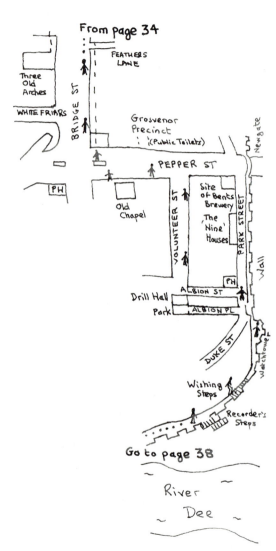

From page 34

FEATHERS LANE

Three Old Arches

WHITE FRIARS

BRIDGE ST

Grosvenor Precinct (Public Toilets)

PEPPER ST

Newgate

VOLUNTEER ST

PARK STREET

Old Chapel

Site of Bent's Brewery

'The 'Nine' Houses'

Wall

PH

Drill Hall

ALBION ST

PH

Park

ALBION PL

DUKE ST

Watchtower

Wishing Steps

Recorder's Steps

Go to page 38

~ River Dee ~

Continue along Bridge Street. Two shops further on look up to your left to the brown oak-timbered frontage of St Michael's Rectory. When the facade of the old building was pulled down in 1974 the contractors found old carvings underneath; these were copied during rebuilding.

Three Old Arches in Bridge Street

FEATHERS LANE 🔵 is one of the four remaining medieval lanes in the city. In the 19th century there was a bridge above it which lifted in two halves to allow coaches through and was nicknamed London Bridge (of course it is Tower Bridge in the Capital that opens but an American company may also have confused the two 'London' bridges when they bought London Bridge in the 1960s and transported it stone by stone to the Nevada Desert.)

CITY guides sometimes show visitors through the last door on the left up Feathers Lane, turning left and going through the next door to give them a surprise — coming out on the row above without appearing to have gone up at all. Unfortunately the way is not public.

AT THE corner of the next road look up to see some strange carved figures on the former Saint Michael's Church. Although a church was here in the 13th century, the most impressive part of the building is the internal chancel roof, thought to date from the 15th century. Most of the church was rebuilt in 1581 and it was enlarged in the mid-19th century. The old west porch can be found preserved in the Grosvenor Park. The church was closed in 1972 and became a Heritage Centre in 1975. The row goes under the church tower making this the only church in the country to have a public path through it. 🔵

Cross the road ahead at the traffic lights then turn left along Pepper Street.

Pass the columns of a large shop on your right. 🔵

HE PROUD lion surveying the city from the top of the car park ahead came from Bents' Brewery which once stood on the same site.

LOOK across the road. The stained glass on the modern Grosvenor Precinct depicts all the Chester gates: it is easier to see them when it is dark and the internal lights are on.

'Seek and ye shall find'.
The front of this former chapel was bricked up and 'lost' for many years

Turn right along Volunteer Street. Continue to the castellated Drill Hall facing you at the end of the street. It was built in 1869 at a cost

LOOK FOR THE BLUE PLAQUE

of approximately £2,500. Now the gates of the hall have been moved back from their original position, the inside opened to the sky, and a tiny park, a quiet place to relax and read, built in what was

Drill Hall

the back yard. (To get to the park legally you have to go around the block.)

Turn left. At the end of the street, stop. Forty metres to your left are the 'Nine houses'. LOOK FOR THE BLUE PLAQUE

Four mirrored pairs and an endhouse were built here in 1650. This design of a solid wall base and timber uppers is rare outside Chester. It is more often seen when the wooden base of a timber-framed house has rotted and been replaced with stone or brick. When building was completed Robert Harvey of the City of London, haberdasher, sold all nine to Randle Stanway of Chester for £230. In 1850 numbers 2 and 4 were made into one house while two houses were demolished. The last six were restored in 1969.

Cross over and turn right along Park Street. At the corner of Albion Street is the pub of the same name. Albion is the earliest name for Britain. Recorded by the Romans, it probably came from the Celtic. The cosy old-fashioned pub features memorabilia from the First World War.

Head up the slope onto the city wall. Continue ahead. The wide area on the wall is a good place to stop for the view - so good in fact that this was where the old watchtower stood.

Go down the 'Wishing Steps'. If you can run up and down them whilst holding your breath, your wish may come true. The original legend only included young women looking for husbands but the tale has grown with the telling.

Ignore the next steps on your left. These are the Recorder's Steps said, by a stone plaque, to have been built for the city Recorder (chairman of the bench or head judge) in 1700 but not completed until 1720, after his death. Chester has had Recorders since the Great Charter of Henry VII created local Quarter Sessions. Since their demise in 1971 an Honorary Recorder has been appointed.

The map (left)

From page 36

LOWER BRIDGE ST.
o Firemark
Bridge-gate
CASTLE DR.
Round Tower Wall
River Dee
OLD DEE BRIDGE
St JOHN'S VIEW
PH
HANDBRIDGE
MILL ST.

Go to page 40

Continue along the wall for 100 metres. Chester Weir is the earliest one recorded in Britain. It was built by the first Earl of Chester who 'erected the causey and granted three score fisheries above the said weir to several of his dependants, commonly called stalls in Dee reserving to himself the Earl's Poole, next to the causey and granted the abbot the tithes of the said mills and fishings.' By the 19th century there were five water-powered mills producing everything from flour and oatmeal to needlepoints and snuff.

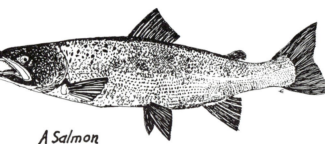

A Salmon

Cormorants, seagulls and a variety of ducks perch on top of the weir when the tide is out, waiting perhaps, for the salmon who use the steps to reach their spawning grounds in the upper reaches of the river. High tides create a bore which runs upriver and hits the weir. The tide then flows over the top carrying flotsam, jetsam and mud to dump on the normally neat and clean walkway below the Victorian bandstand. The

---

tide can reach Holt, ten miles upstream. It sometimes brings with it the occasional seal or the 'miraculous fish' recorded in the 17th century.

Beside the remains of the Rou Tower fork right, down the slope to street level. A few houses uphill is a firemark from the Sun Company. **See Firefighters feature.**

Sun Firemark

17.10

Turn downhill and go through the pedestrian arch of the Bridgegate. The earlier gate included a water tower on the battlements which stored and fed water to the city. At the beginning of the 17th century the tower was filled by one of the first water engines which used river water as a source of energy to pump more water to the top of the tower. The first square tower was damaged in the Civil War, then an octagonal one was erected with new works in 1692. The city had been without a piped water supply for 45 years (except for a pump in 16?

LOOK FOR THE BLUE PLAQUE

Daniel Defoe, author of 'Robinson Crusoe', described the problem in his 'Tour Thro' the Whole Island of Great Britain'. '...in the city, about 1690, they had no water to supply their ordinary occasions but what was carried from the River Dee upon horses in great leather vessels.'

The carving of 1714 was on the old Bridgegate.

A stone carving commemorating the investiture of the Prince of Wales is set in the city wall. The 'Feathers' emblem is surrounded by the motto of the Most Noble Order of the Garter.

Head across the Old Dee Bridge.
The Norman Domesday Book of 1086 records how 'one man sent from each hide [approx. 50 hectares] of land to repair the bridge and walls. If he failed to come his lord paid 40s'. In 1227 the bridge 'wasted away', and in 1279 a later bridge was washed away. It was replaced in 1280 by a part-timber, part-stone bridge. In 1357 the Mayor and Commonality were ordered to repair the bridge in stone 'as per the rest of the bridge'.

Traffic over the bridge was regulated by tolls, by ordinance (bye-law) and for defence. In 1241 the bridge keepers could take, for example, 'of every carte entringe with herringes, tenne herringes and of every horselode fyve ... And of every lode nuttes three handfull'. The keepers had duties, 'to fynde lockes with keyes at twoe gates, that is to say at the said gate of the bridge shipgate and at the horsegate [the horsegate or caplegate led to the river for watering horses] and one man allwais to keep the said gate of the bridge to shutt and open'.

In 1533 Henry ap Res allowed carts with iron wheels to cross the bridge against ordinance but was pardoned by the mayor. In 1574 defensive measures on the bridge included 'in the middle thereof a gate of lern which in the night was taken up'.

The bridge was widened in 1826 by Thomas Harrison, with iron railings placed on the upstream side. However the downstream side remains much as it was in the 14th century with 'refuges' for pedestrians to avoid pack animals, carts and cattle.

At the far end of the bridge cross the road by the traffic light to St John's View.

Randle Holmes' sketch of the Dee Bridge includes the square 'Tyrer's Tower' atop the old Bridgegate.

The grey tollgate post still stands beside the road.
Toll Fees (abolished on the 1st January 1885) included:

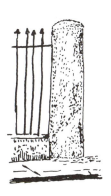

Carriage or Gig	9d
Wagon or Cart	6d
Saddle Horse	2d
Cattle (each)	1d

WALK

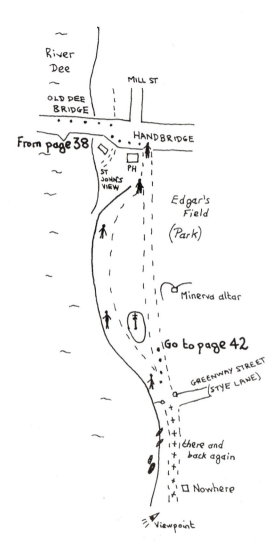

~ River Dee ~

MILL ST

OLD DEE BRIDGE

From page 38

HANDBRIDGE

PH

ST JOHN'S VIEW

Edgar's Field (Park)

Minerva altar

Go to page 42

GREENWAY STREET (STYE LANE)

there and back again

☐ Nowhere

Viewpoint

Pass the Ship Inn and turn right into the park.

THE SHIP INN

The Ship Inn

Fork right and follow the riverside walk. A rock shelf, used for centuries as a ford, can still be seen below the park wall when the river is low. The Roman bridge probably lay between here and the present bridge. Even with the bridge in place, people walked across the river as late as the 19th century, presumably to avoid the bridge toll. Unfortunately the

Entrance to the park (Edgar's Field)

records for these crossings are the coron inquests for the unlucky few who we swept away by the strong current.

there and back again
At the end of the park you can extend the walk along the river-bank to get a view of the Grosvenor Bridge and the salmon fishing boats. Greenway Street (Stye Lane) to your left has been the home of fishermen through the centuries. Whil waiting for the boats to come in, childrer carved graffiti of boats and lorries int the park's sandstone walls. **When you decide, in 400 metres or so, that you are getting Nowhere, return to the park to continue the wal**

NOWHERE

When the owners of two new cottages gave their addresses as 1 and 2 Nowhere, the owner of Nowhere took them to court. The judge ruled that only he lived Nowhere.

CIVIL WAR

1640
Sep 18 City watch continued at night.
Oct 15 Assembly members ordered to provide muskets, calivers, corselets and halberds. *'in these warrlike and dangerous times'* Eastgate and Bridgegate to be repaired and a new gate to be fitted in the Newgate.
Jan 1 Murengers request money for wall repairs.

1642
Aug 8 Great 'tumult' caused by drum beaten by direction of Sir William Brereton MP. His men imprisoned, his house burnt, he evicted.
Aug 22 *King Charles I raises standard at Nottingham.*
Sep 6 100 marks assessed on citizens for wall repairs as *'present and imminent dangers... are upon the land'.* Shot and powder bought.
Sep 23 King Charles I visits Chester. Given 100 lbs gold.
Oct 21 300 inhabitants raised and armed with muskets as well as the trained band.
Nov 11 At six gates 8 guards - 4 with muskets, 4 with halberds. Twelve man guard at High Cross.
Feb 3 £100 levied on inhabitants for fortifications. *'that wee shall all joyne together in a mutuall Association for the defence of this Citty against all Forces whatsoever....hostile'*
* The New Year was on March 25th 'til 1752.

1643
Jul 18 Brereton's Parliamentary forces attack. 2 Royalist youths shot on walls.
Jul 21 Brereton retreats to Tarvin.

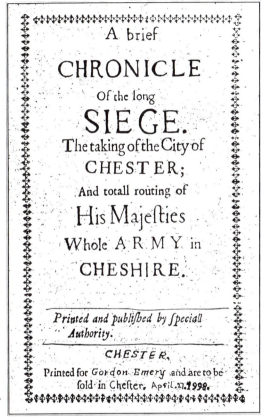

A brief

CHRONICLE

Of the long

SIEGE.

The taking of the City of

CHESTER;

And totall routing of

His Majesties

Whole A R M Y in

CHESHIRE.

Printed and published by speciall Authority.

CHESTER,

Printed for *Gordon Emery* and are to be sold in Chester. April 17 1998.

Design based on pamphlets of the period

Jul 25 City fires barns outside Boughton.
Oct 20 Robert Grosvenor authorised to enclose row in his house. Three troop of horse to be raised.
Nov 11 Nearby Hawarden Castle captured for Parl't.
Dec 1 Lord Byron reaches Chester for King.

Dec 1 £100 City plate to be melted. Parliament troops encircle city.
Dec 6 Royalists recapture Hawarden.
Feb 19 - Mar 13 Maurice relieves Chester.

1644
Jul 25 Prince Rupert at Chester makes Lord Byron Governor.
December Siege resumed. Chester encircled.

1645
May Relief army from Oxford diverted to Naseby.
May 8 *'no fresh meate and little fish'* in city. No provisions within 8-10 miles for the Parliamentary besiegers.
Jun 13 Brereton called to London to answer charges of: 1) not carrying out proper works 2) soldiers not doing duty 3) looting Wales.
Sep 20 Eastern suburbs captured by Parl't.
Sep 21 King advances to relieve city.
Sep 23 King Charles arrives in Chester.
Sep 24 Battle of Rowton Heath. Royalist army routed. Charles watches the remnants of his forces fighting in the suburbs from the Phoenix Tower, then moves to the Cathedral Tower where the Captain beside him is shot through the head with a musket ball fired from St. John's Church tower.
Nov 28 Brereton writes, *'The beseiged in Chester remain obstinate'.*
Dec 10 Brereton's mortar attacks described as, *'great grenadoes like so many demi-phaetons threaten to set the city if not the world alight'.*
Dec 30 Brereton reports complete encirclement.
Feb 3 Lord Byron surrenders Chester.

feature

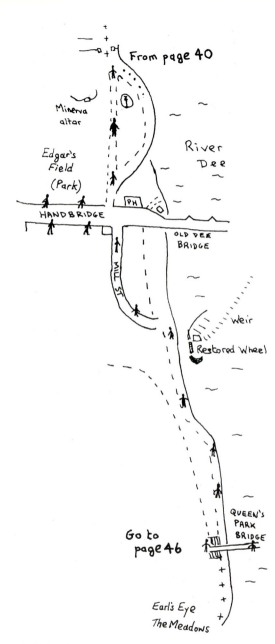

From page 40

Minerva altar

Edgar's Field (Park)

River Dee

HANDBRIDGE

PH

OLD DEE BRIDGE

MILL ST

Weir

Restored Wheel

Go to page 46

QUEEN'S PARK BRIDGE

Earl's Eye The Meadows

Return through the park on the upper path.

An ornate iron pole on top of the rock to your left marks and ventilates a Victorian sewer.

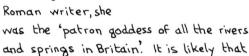

Sewer Vent

IN THE rock on your right is a unique Roman carving of the goddess Minerva. According to a Roman writer, she was the 'patron goddess of all the rivers and springs in Britain'. It is likely that travellers wishing to cross the river paid homage here. In later times St Mary was worshipped in a similar way. (At Holt, upstream, the ancient bridge had a chapel dedicated to St Mary in

Minerva with her owl at the shrine

the middle.) Historians suggest, after the Roman period ended, people thought Minerva was a carving of St Mary and not realising that it was a pagan symbol, did not destroy it.

STONES from a ruin have been removed from the park which suggests that there may have been a chapel here. However the park's name, Edgar's Field comes from the legend that King Edgar the Pacific had a palace here in the tenth century where he began his historic journey upriver

Continue to the road and turn right.

Opposite are neat half-timbered houses dated by the postbox in the Post Office wall. The street and the suburb are named Handbridge. The name comes from Honebruge (stone bridge or one bridge, C13th). In the Civil War a diarist records that, 'Handbridge was made another treboeth [burnt town] being burnt by the command of the Governor Lord Byron to prevent their nesting others'.

Cross the road using the pedestrian lights. Turn left towards the river then, at the black and white corner building, turn right along Mill St. Continue along the riverside path.

...ne 1960's flats, possibly the ugliest archi-
...ecture in the city, are on the site of a
Roman quarry.

Looking across at the Bridgegate.

STANDING out in the river, in 1355, were
...ulling mills used for processing woollen
...loth. By 1698 one had been converted
...o paper-making, and by 1701 there was
... snuff (powdered tobacco) mill on the site.
...ook for the restored mill wheel at this
...nd of the weir.

Continue to the suspension bridge.

there and back again

If you continue along the riverside path you will come to the
Meadows. This area of meadowland
is also known as Earl's Eye (island).
An old manuscript states that, 'The
river of Dee was drawn unto the said
cittie with great charge by the said
Earle [Hugh] or some of his predecessors
before the Conquest, from the antiente
course which it held before, a myle or two
distant from the cittie, and a passage
cut out of rock under the walls of the
said cittie?'

In Roman times the river was not
always navigable and they may have had
to carry bricks, which they made ten
miles upstream at Holt (BOVIVM), overland.
It seems that the Normans overcame
this problem and may have joined this
island to Handbridge in the process, as
well as supplying a good head of water
for their new weir.

**The path can be followed as far
as you like. In three miles is the
unspoilt village of Eccleston.
Return to the suspension bridge
to continue the main walk.**

River Cruise Boat on the Dee

Queen's Park Suspension Bridge

Cross the Queen's Park Bridge.

This is the second suspension bridge
here. The first, built in 1852, was private.
Appropriately the contractor was a Mr
Dredge.

SHIELDS of Chester's seven Norman
earls can be seen on the towers.
See feature. It is, perhaps, ironic that
the wheatsheaf on Chester's coat of arms
comes from Earl Randle or Ranulph (1120).
He used three wheatsheafs on his armorial
crest, and yet it was he who destroyed
all the Wirral farms, replacing them with
a hunting forest.

NORMAN EARLS

WILLIAM the Conqueror gave Chester to the Flemish noble Gherbaud, but he returned to Flanders where he was killed.

HUGH LUPUS   1071-1101

It was William's nephew Hugo d'Avranches that became Chester's first Norman earl. As well as controlling huge estates in England, Hugo or Hugh was a Marcher lord: he had to respect his English boundaries but he could take as much of North Wales as he could hold. Hugh had his own court, he made his own laws and issued his own charters. However, in taking Chester, the Norman army had destroyed nearly half the houses and laid waste surrounding villages. The earl had to rebuild the city, keep the border secure and, with the help of his barons, ensure the smooth-running of estates in England and Normandy.

He is described as having a 'retinue more like an army than a household'. He kept large hunting forests to the east of Chester and 'preferred falconers and huntsmen to the cultivators of the soil and ministers of heaven'. His wolf standard gave him the name 'Hugo de lou' (Hugh the wolf) but he also 'took great pleasure in gaming and debauchery' and became so overweight he earned the Welsh name 'Hugh Vras' (Hugh the fat).

In 1092(3), perhaps worried about his unholy life, he founded St. Werburgh's Abbey and finally became a monk just a few days before he died.

Hugh Lupus Shield on Queen's Park Bridge

RICHARD   1101-1120

Richard was seven when he inherited his father's vast estates and so Henry I became his guardian. He was educated with the King's children in France. At the age of 26 he set sail for England with William, the King's son and heir. The sailors carrying these nobles celebrated with three hogsheads (large casks) of wine and, perhaps because of this, the 'White Ship' ran aground and sank. Both nobles and all but one of the court and crew drowned.

RANULPH (Meschines) 1120-1129

The nephew of Hugh Lupus, Ranulph, gave some of his lands to the King upon inheriting Chester, only to win some back when his stepson rebelled against the King in Normandy. He converted the Wirral farmlands into a hunting forest.

Norman Falconry

RANULP II (Gernons) 1129-1153

Ranulph II, Ranulph's son, tried to reclaim the northern estates and extend his lands into Lincoln. To this end he supported Matilda against Stephen, both fighting for the English throne. After helping to capture Stephen near Lincoln (Stephen was later ransomed) he became a neutral as Matilda's power waned. Nevertheless Stephen took revenge and captured the

...rl, only releasing him for the return of ...astles and land. As soon as he was ...ee, Ranulph turned against Stephen ...d eventually gained large estates ...suring that the earldom held nearly ... third of England.

...owever, while supporting the next ...ing, Henry, he was 'poisoned using ...itchcraft' by William Peverill whose ...nds he had been offered as a reward.

...UGH II (Gyffylliog) 1153-1181
...ugh, born at Cyffylliog near Ruthin, ...upported the son of Henry II as he ...ought against his father. For this he ...as imprisoned but later released ...nd given back his lands.

...ANULPH III (Blundeville) 1181-1232
...Blonde Ville, a monastery in Oswestry ...as this earl's birthplace. He married ...o become son-in-law of Henry II and ...rother-in-law of Richard (I the Lionheart). ...n 1216 he became the Earl of Lincoln. ...uring 1218 he made a treaty with the ...elsh prince Llewelyn before he went off ...o the Crusades. On his return he built ...eeston Castle. At his death he had ...is heart interred at Dieulacres Abbey ...n Staffordshire which he founded. ...is body remained in Chester.

JOHN THE SCOT 1232-1237
John became the earl by right of male succession but only inherited a small portion of his uncle's lands which were divided amongst Ranulph III's sisters and great neices. His co-heirs sued to partition his lands but he died without children before legal action was completed.

THE EARLDOM reverted to the Crown. King Henry III gave it to his son Edward (later Edward I).

Building a Norman Motte (wooden castle)
From the Bayeux Tapestry

Right: The Laws, Taxes and Fines of the City of Chester before 1066 (Domesday Book 1086) Edited.

CIVITAS DE CESTRE
(THE CITY OF CHESTER)

Paid tax on 50 hides (about 200 hectares) There were 431 taxed houses plus the Bishop's 56. The City paid 10½ silver marks.

Those breaching the King's peace were fined 100s. If a free man murdered, he was outlawed, goods taken. Whoever shed blood from Monday to Saturday noon fined 10s. On weekends or holy days 20s. Whoever killed a man on a holyday £4 others £2. Burglary or robbery: Holydays £4 others £2. Collusion with a thief: Fine 10s. Robbery, theft or violence to a woman in a house: £2 each offence. Unlawful intercourse: by a widow 20s, by a girl 10s. Theft of Land: 40s. Land claims for self or kin: 10s. Unclaimed Land confiscated. Tax evasion: 10s. Letting fire start in city: 3d, and 2s to neighbour. Two-thirds of fines go to the king, ⅓ to earl. Ships docking illegally. 40s from each man. Ship breaking the peace, ship+crew confiscated. Shipping Tolls 4d per cargo. Marten skins offered to king's reeve first on pain of fine 40s. False measure of ale: 4s fine. Bad ale: maker in cucking stool or 4s fine.

feature

From page 42

QUEEN'S PARK BRIDGE

~ River Dee ~

THE GROVES

Bandstand

Rock House (The Anchorite Cell)

Grosvenor Park

← St John's Trail

St John's Church

Go to page 48

Amphitheatre

VICARS LANE

LITTLE ST JOHN ST

i

Chester Visitor Centre

DIRECTLY ahead of the bridge is the entrance to Grosvenor Park.

Arch from St Mary's Nunnery in the park

You may like to wander around or just sit in the relative peace of the formal gardens. A hundred metres or so inside the park is the old Shipgate, rebuilt here alongside the porch of St. Michael's Church and an arch from St. Mary's Nunnery. The grounds also contain a Sicilian marble statue of the Second Marquis of Westminster who donated the park to the city in 1867. A lodge displays statuettes of William the Conqueror and Chester's Norman earls. There is also a duck pond, a scented garden for the blind, and a playground.

Second Marquis of Westminster

From the bridge turn left, along the riverside. Up on a sandstone roc is the 'Anchorite Cell', now a private hou

The Anchorite Cell

A Chester legend tells that King Harold, after losing the Battle of Hast came here, mortally wounded in one e and died here as a hermit in the Anchorite Cell before William finally took Chester in 1069. The fact that Harol wife came to Chester has given the legend some credence.

The bandstand at The Groves

Turn right up steps opposite the bandstand, completed for £350. The Mounted Band of the Royal Artillery was the first band to play here on the 7th May 1913.

Stop at the top of the steps. St John's Church is on your right. In the tenth century an earlier building was used in the Service of Fealty or loyalty from the eight princes in Britain who accepted King Edgar as their liege.

St John's was Chester's only cathedral in Norman times. The building is now half the original size, although the ruins still remain. The great tower, captured by the Parliamentarians in the Civil War and fitted with a 'platform for musketry and small arms' after it was captured, fell down with an enormous crash over 200 years later, at the end of the 19th century.

The ruins of St Johns Church from the NE.

When the gates are open on your right, you may like to follow St John's Trail around the church before continuing.

A roof 'boss' found in the ruins is the inspiration for the metal trail plaques.

The trail features metal plaques outside the church and there are display boards within. Both give the history of this ancient site. Curiously the eight princes or kings who rowed Edgar up the Dee have now increased to twelve.

Continue to the main road.
Opposite is the Chester Visitor Centre. Information, crafts and refreshments can be found within. Mind the traffic if you cross here; pedestrian lights can be found a hundred metres further on.

Turn left through the remains of the Roman amphitheatre.

The Roman Amphitheatre

The small altar to Nemesis in the northern entrance (the original is at the Grosvenor Museum) was set up by Centurion Marcianus after a vision.

WALK

Nemesis was the goddess of retribution and justice.

Altar to Nemesis found in the Roman Amphitheatre

Did Sextus Marcianus have a score to settle or were his moral standards high? Either way it is likely that many of the criminals executed here in the ring would have believed that their guilty souls would be transported to Tartarus (Hades or Hell).

Tile found near the Amphitheatre

In Rome, at Titus' inauguration in AD8 the slaughter went on for 100 days wi 9,000 animals killed as well as thousa of men and women. No-one knows ho many criminals were executed here, outside the fortress of DEVA (Chester) or how many gladiators fought to th death in this oval theatre of blood

Opposite are pretty almshouses (187

Leave the amphitheatre by the far entrance. Cross Souters Lane on your left and pass the Roman Gardens, a small park. Columns, column bases and th base pillars of hypocausts, dug up at various times around the city, have been placed here for preservation.

THIS WAS once the site of a brick and tile cockpit building put up in 1825 to replace a thatched one. It cost five shillings to visit. There was a

From page 46

St John's Church

VICARS LANE

SOUTERS LANE

Roman Gardens

PARK ST

Chester Visitor Centre

LUMLEY PL.

LITTLE ST JOHN STREET

Amphitheatre

Altar

New-gate

Park

Wolf-gate

Almshouses

ST JOHN STREET

Grosvenor Precinct

Wall

EASTGATE STREET...

Eastgate

Go to page 52

Cockpit Hill near Frodsham Street as well. In 1754, pupils of the King's School had to pay two shillings and six pence a term to their headmaster towards cocks for the 'sport'. Cockfighting was also an added attraction at the Chester Races.

Columns in the Roman Gardens

Go through the Newgate, turn immediately left along Park Street and immediately left again up the steps to the wall. It was in this vicinity, on dark nights in the 19th century, that the Newgate Ghost walked. It grew taller as one watched. One woman was so frightened that she persuaded her brave husband to chase it. He caught it — and found a baker's wife under a sheet. She had a broom which raised the sheet to make her appear taller. After being admonished she promised not to

'haunt' anyone again.

The Wolfgate or Peppergate
(the original Newgate)

Cross the modern Newgate and the Wolfgate. The modern Newgate dates to 1938 but the Wolfgate is the oldest remaining gate in the city wall, rebuilt in 1608. The name may come from the Norse personal name 'Ulfaldi': in 1303 it was recorded as 'Wolfuldsgate'. However, it is also said that there was a wolf's head carving above the old gate and, as this was the coat of arms of the Norman earl, Hugh Lupus (the wolf), that the gate was named after him.

BESIDE the gate, in the park below, is the

base of the Roman Southeast Angle Tower, once inside, but now outside the wall which was moved in medieval times.

Pass Thimbleby's Tower. Partially destroyed in the Civil War, it may have been named after Sir Richard Thimblebye of Hilbre Island or Lady Thimbleby who died in Chester in 1615. The tower has only recently been reroofed in a mock-medieval style.

Follow the wall over the Eastgate under the clock. *See Feature.* When the old gate was demolished in 1768, parts of the Roman gate, the Porta Principalis Sinastra, were found incorporated in the stonework. Here the wall is nearer its original Roman course.

Descend the steps on your right. At street level go through the Eastgate. LOOK FOR THE BLUE PLAQUE

A TRAMWAY bracket has been re-used by the Chester Grosvenor Hotel to stop their sign swinging. Other brackets can be seen further along the street, reminders of the electric trams that ran to the railway station from April 1903 until February 1930 when they were replaced with buses.

WALK

The Eastgate, Chester, 1903

Electric trams ran from April 1903 until February 1930. The Eastgate Clock had been erected in 1899. Great Western Railway wagons collected and delivered to Chester Railway Station (opened 1847). Chester Northgate Brewery Company, trading from 1864, had retail premises in Foregate Stre

feature

The Eastgate Clock

The ornamental clock on the Eastgate is not Chester's only visible clock or even the oldest but it is the most famous. Its grand design is by Douglas and Minshull, local architects who, on behalf of the Duke of Westminster, came up with the first plans to improve the Eastgate in 1884. John Douglas's original plan was for a clock in stonework but it was agreed that this would contravene the law of 'ancient lights', blocking daylight to nearby properties.

By 1897 subscribers had donated money for several schemes to commemorate Queen Victoria's Jubilee. Colonel Edward Evans-Lloyd, a local solicitor, fed up with the length of time the project was taking, offered to pay for all the clock mechanism. James Swindley, a cousin of Douglas and blacksmith in Handbridge, accepted the commission for the intricate frame. Inscription panels representing the emblems of England, Scotland, Wales and Ireland were made by the Coalbrookdale Iron Company.

Finally by the 21st May 1899 the clock stood above the Eastgate.

James Joyce of Whitchurch had made the inner workings — a pinwheel deadbeat mechanism kept going by a pendulum weighing over a hundredweight (50k).

However the original idea had been to celebrate Queen Victoria's Jubilee and this had already taken place on 20th June 1897 with processions, flags and a 60 gun salute in the Castle yard. That evening two thousand pensioners had been treated to a 'meat tea' in the Town Hall and were given presents: 2 ounces of tobacco for the men, ½ pound of tea for the women. The River Dee had displayed 'God Save The Queen' banners on the shore, some illuminated by Chinese lanterns and 'beautiful coloured miniature lights' on the suspension bridge whilst a floating convoy of steamers, barges and boats sailed past.

So instead, the clock's starting date was set for Queen Victoria's 80th birthday on 27th May 1899. At 12.45 the clock ticked for the first time. Until 1973 the firm of James Joyce wound the clock each week, then electric winding was introduced. In 1992 the whole mechanism was replaced by an electric one. Nowadays, visitors use over a tonne of paper each year for prints of Chester's Eastgate Clock.

Continue along Eastgate Street.

TWELVE shields of the counties of Wales (before 1974 reorganisation) adorn the building beside the Eastgate, built in 188 and enlarged in 1908 by John Douglas. Look too for the stone memorial to Owen Jones, a local butcher, who bequeathed his land to 'the poor of every Company of Merchants and Craftsmen of Chester.' The charity's funds escalated when lead mines were dug on its land at

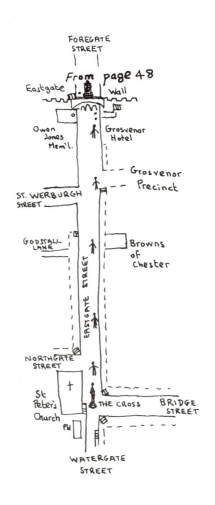

From page 48

FOREGATE STREET

Eastgate / Wall

Owen Jones Mem'l. / Grosvenor Hotel

ST. WERBURGH STREET

Grosvenor Precinct

GODSTALL LANE

Browns of Chester

EASTGATE STREET

NORTHGATE STREET

St Peter's Church

PH

THE CROSS / BRIDGE STREET

WATERGATE STREET

Owen Jones Memorial

East side of Saint Werburgh Street

LOOK FOR THE BLUE PLAQUE

Minera in North Wales; a pub there is till named the City Arms.

FURTHER along Eastgate Street, local architect Thomas Penson, a student Thomas Harrison, designed Browns of Chester in the Greek Revivalist style in 1828. Next door, the High Gothic 'Crypt buildings' with their quirky gables and tower date from 1858.

Crown and Glove sign

THE CROWN and glove sign was from a former public house.

Another hand or glove, made of wood, once hung from the corner of St Peter's Church roof — until 1803 it had been above George Lowe's shop on Pentice Row — for 14 days before each of the two annual fairs. It had been hung from medieval times as a symbol of the king's peace (although in Chester it was the earl's peace). Even felons could come to the city during the fairs without threat of imprisonment unless they commited further crimes while they were here.

However, in 1836, the new mayor refused to pay Peter Catherall, the clerk, his fee for looking after the wooden hand, telling him it was 'a foolish old custom' and he could 'do what he liked' with the artefact. It was sold for 'two pints of ale' at the 'Sign of the Boot'. The ancient symbol ended up in Liverpool Museum. During the bombing raids of World War II it was destroyed.

Front
HUGO COMES
CESTRIA (Hugh
Earl of Chester)
Reverse
GUILDA DE
CIVIT. MERCAL
MCCIX (Guild
Merchant of
the city 1159

Chester Hand or Glove

Your return to the Cross ends this section of the walk. You can start on the next section or refresh yourself in one of Chester's many fine cafés, pubs or restaurants.

Browns of Chester

WALK

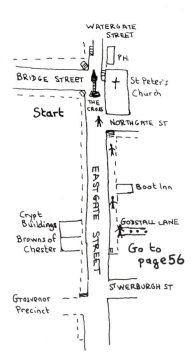

WATERGATE STREET

P.H.

BRIDGE STREET

St Peter's Church

THE CROSS

Start

NORTHGATE ST

Boot Inn

EASTGATE STREET

Crypt Buildings

Browns of Chester

GODSTALL LANE

Go to page 56

Grosvenor Precinct

ST WERBURGH ST

SECTION 3   2.9 Km

Cathedral
NORTHEAST QUARTER OF CHESTER

Start this section of the walk at the Cross. St Peter's Church tower had the first public clock in the city. A working clock was erected in 1585 and by 1612 it was striking the quarter hour. A new clock was put up in 1813. Nowadays it is the ornamental clock on the Eastgate that is more prominent.

Walk towards the Eastgate Clock but in only 20 metres ascend the steps, on your left, onto the Eastgate Row and continue ahead. The stalls and shops on the outside once completely enclosed this row, so that it became known as Dark Row. As early as 1280 there were 'Buttershoppes' here. In 1488 there was a reference to the 'Botershoppez alias dicta le Dirke Loftez in le Eskgate strete', and in 1581, 'The Butter Shops next the Milk Shops'. In 1630 a lease enabled Sir Ranulph Crewe to enter 'any those Sevrall Shoppes comonly

called the Buttershops', if his rent was unpaid. By 1635 another deed includes 'buildings near to the Milkstoopes... together with all singular Edifices, buildings, rooms, sellars, Sollars [bedrooms] Shops, Stalls, lights, wayes, howes, easmer proffitts, commodities and Adva[n]tages whatsoever'. The owner was obviously trying to cover any eventuality.

Eastgate Row was 'Dark Row'

THE BOOT INN is said to have been built in 1643 with timbers of Spanish oak from dismantled galleons. In fact, the wood is more likely to have been taken from houses outside the city that were knocked down for defensive measures in the Civil War. Look for the musket ball, behind the bar, taken out of a joist during restoration work. The inn was used as a meeting place by the Royalist troops besieged in the city.

In the rear bar is the horsetraders' box where the dealers would discuss prices at the Chester Horsemarket. Curtains which assured privacy have long since gone. The Assembly Book minutes for 6th January 1704 record, 'It is ordered that the horse fair shall be kept for the future in the fforegate street of this City and in no other place, and that publick notice thereof be posted up in due tyme before the next ffair; and that the ffurther Northgate Street be the fixt place for the beast markett: and that the Clothmarket be continued in the Bridge Street where itt now is and not removed to any other place.'

At night, it is said, the 'ladies' would use the horse traders' box and pull the curtains closed to discuss their prices.

The High Gothic 'Crypt Buildings'

The City Assembly w already aware of Chester's reputation, for as early as the mid-16th century a byelaw proclaimed that, 'wher as all the tavernes and ale housis of this citie have and be used to be kept by young women, otherwise then is used in eny other places of this relme, wherof all strangers resorting hether greatly marvil and thinke it an unconvenyent use, wherby not onely grete slaunder and dishonest report of this citie hath and doth run a brode... it is ordered... that no tavarns nor ale-houses be kept... by eny women being

betwene fourteen and forty yeres of age?

Three bays beyond the Boot Inn, and opposite the High Gothic 'Crypt Buildings', turn left along a small passageway: Godstall Lane.

The name Godstall or Godescal comes from a Chester legend. An unnamed tomb painted with golden eagles in the southeast aisle of the cathedral is said

Godstall Lane

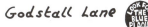

WALK

From page 54

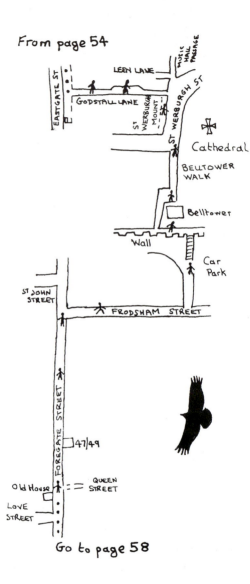

Go to page 58

to be the tomb of the Holy Roman Emperor (Emperor of Aquitaine) Henry V, who named himself Godescallus and is said to have spent his last years as a hermit in this city. Other records show that Henry V died elsewhere, leaving the legend, the tomb, and the identity of the hermit a mystery.

This lane was also once known as Bakers' Entry and was the site of the medieval St Giles' Bakery. But this passageway

St Werburgh Mount

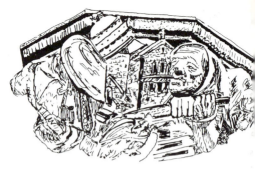

Carved Heads: Gladstone

has an even older history: it was the la alongside the *praetorium* or Legates Palace in the Roman Fortress.

At the end of the lane turn right under the overhanging buildings of St Werburgh Mount, then cross the road to the telephone box. Look at the carved heads on the corner of the Cathedral above the 'Garden of Remembrance' sign. Some are caricatures of political figures from t 19th century: Disraeli holds a sword, Gladstone a pen.

LOOK FOR THE BLUE PLAQUE

THE Garden of Remembrance is for soldi who fought in the Second World War. book of names for those who died, serving in the 22nd Cheshire Regiment, can be found in the Cathedral. The garden was redesigned in 1997 to present a medal and ribbon. The pattern best seen from the city wall.

...eep the Victorian letterbox on ...our right and go along the ...assage: Belltower Walk. The slated ...uilding of 1975 was the first English ...eestanding belltower built since the ...iddle Ages.

...HE FIRST ravens to nest in any English ...ty centre since the Middle Ages took ...heir fancy to a stone gargoyle on ...is side of the Cathedral in 1997 after ...esting on the Town Hall the previous ...ear. Listen for their hoarse 'kraa-...raa-kraa' calls.

...urn left along the wall. In 1815 ...e walls were crowded every night here ...s people stood and listened to the ...dreadful sounds' of 'apparently ...nguished spirits' which seemed to come ...om the steeple. It was eventually ...scovered that two owls had taken ...p residence.

...urn immediately right down the ...irst stone steps. Look to your right ...o see the foundations of the Roman ...all, building started around 102AD.

...t the T-junction turn right

beside the mock-Roman pillars of a modern shopping parade. Turn left at the next T-junction into Foregate Street. Roman pavements have been discovered nearly two metres below the present street.

Carved head

LESS than 100 metres along, look for the carved figures on number 47/49, once the Old Nag's Head Inn. The date of 1592 (said to be a wild guess by the architect at the time of rebuilding) is carved near the roof.

OVER the road was Ye Olde Royal Oak Hotel. This popular pub name refers to the oak in which King Charles II hid from his enemies. A lease of 1674 states that the pub was formerly called The Raven.

Pass the Old Queen's Head. Do you know how many English queens were decapitated? Three in the 16th

Old house in Foregate Street

century as well as Mary, Queen of Scots. Here though, the name refers to a picture of Queen Victoria.

AT THE END of the street take a peek down Bath Street on your right: John Douglas built the French Chateau style houses, with their characteristic round towers and spires, in 1903 — one of the more interesting designs in the city.

WALK

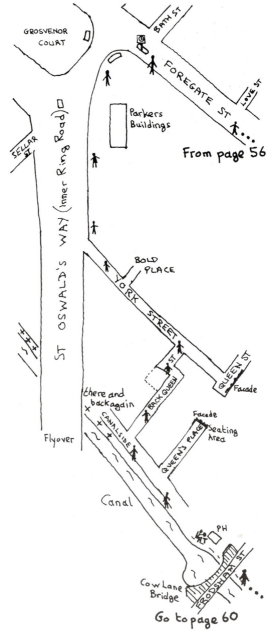

From page 56

Go to page 60

Houses
in Bath Street

At the freestanding clock, opposite the built up roundabout, turn Left.

As you follow the main road around to your Left, Parker's Buildings, distinguished by their yellow and red brickwork, are on your left. In fact this is a single building of 1889 for retired workers from the Duke of Westminster's Eaton Estate just outside Chester. This early tenement was recently saved from demolition by a housing association.

Turn left along York Street.

Ahead are the Doric pillars of Thomas Harrison's Greek Revival style, Congregational Church, now just the rear wall of a supermarket.

Turn first right to reach the still, murky waters of the Shropshire Union Canal.

Look to your right to see the Mill Hotel and the Steam Mill, now converted to a popular pub and offices.

Former advert on the Steam Mill

THE LEADSHOT Tower behind the Mill is the oldest in the country. Built in 1800 with a third of a million bricks and weighing over 1200 tonnes, it was used to make shot for the Napoleonic War. In a method that is still the cheapest way to produce leadshot, molten lead is poured through a sieve from the top. By the time it reaches a vat of cold water at the bottom, the metal has solidified into near perfect spheres. It is then graded and sorted for a variety of uses.

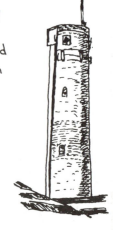

Leadshot Tower

there and back again

Walk as far as you wish along the canal towpath to your right, returning to this point to continue the main route.

The Water Storage Tower

After only a mile the canal reaches the leafy suburbs, a pleasant walk on a warm day, with narrowboats cruising gently past and canalside pubs in half-a-mile and two miles.

Moored up for the night

For the main route turn left and continue along the canal towpath towards the city. At the end of Queen's Place, on your left, is the facade of the school formerly attached to the Congregational Church, rebuilt at 90 degrees to its original site. Beside the facade are shaded seats, ideal for a quiet rest.

AT one time the canalside was a busy industrial part of the city. A wide area of water is now just a 'winding hole' or turning bay. Once it was the entrance to a short arm leading to a Customs & Excise warehouse. The pub is on the site of a timber yard which regularly shipped in supplies of Swedish pine up the River Dee and then by 'flat' barge to the wharf.

C19th Lithograph 'Chester Cathedral'
shows Cowlane Bridge

Cow Lane Bridge

Go under Cow Lane Bridge.

This was used by farmers bringing their animals for sale to the Beast Market at nearby Gorsestacks. In 1818 it was decided that the Cattle Market held weekly in Upper Northgate Street 'to *the inconvenience of residents and coaches to and from Liverpool and Parkgate*' was to be removed to 'Gorse Stacks'. (The area, now a car park, was once where bakers had to store their bread oven fuel.)

Trying to cross Cow Lane Bridge when driven herds were also crossing was a difficult business. Sometimes the occasional cow would leave the herd and wander off to explore one of Chester's shops to the consternation of the proprietor.

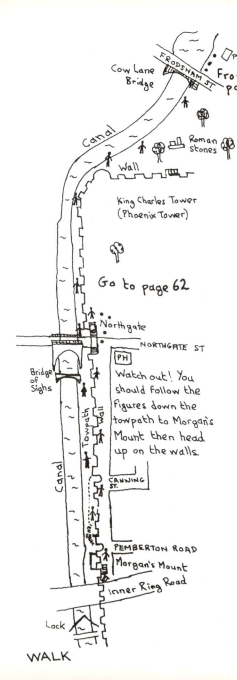

From page 58

Cow Lane Bridge

FRODSHAM ST

PH

Canal

Roman stones

Wall

King Charles Tower (Phoenix Tower)

Go to page 62

Northgate

NORTHGATE ST

PH

Bridge of Sighs

Watch out! You should follow the figures down the towpath to Morgan's Mount then head up on the walls.

Towpath

Wall

Canal

CANNING ST.

PEMBERTON ROAD

Morgan's Mount

Inner Ring Road

Lock

WALK

Pied Wagtail

Motacilla alba yarrellii

Continue along the towpath and you find yourself below the city walls. High above you is the Phoenix or King Charles' Tower, which you will see more of later. Beside you, on the sandstone rock face, are the score marks made by the ropes of horses towing canal boats. Just between the corners are a set of 'pudlocks' designed to hold wooden scaffolding called 'put ups'. A set dating to the 13th century can be found in Caernarvon Castle but it is not known whether these in Chester date from the same period, used for a repair to the city walls. Alternatively they may have been used for '*the Quarry near the Phoenix Tower*' mentioned in 1711, or perhaps from ramps when cutting the canal. When contractors in the late 18th century were paid to excavate the channel through rock they found, to their profit, that there was no rock but just the Roman fosse and the Medieval ditch filled by centuries of rubbish tipped over the city walls — a practice which is unfortunately continued by some who have never heard the phrase : only louts drop litter.

Each Easter volunteers from the local Inland Waterways Association clear the accumulated litter from the canal.

Pass under Northgate Bridge. There was a bridge over the ditch here before the canal. In 1569 the City Treasurers spent £4. 3s. 2d, '*For making the north-gate bridge new, grette joists thick planks*.'

THE small bridge, a little further on, was built in 1793, complete with iron railings, by Joseph Turner for £10. Prisoners from the Northgate Gaol, which stood up to your left, used it for

Bridge of Sighs From above

ccess to the chapel and the 'apartment
ade for prisoners' in the Bluecoat
ospital on the other side. Known as
e 'Bridge of Sighs' or 'Bridge of Death',
was used by those condemned to die,
fter their final visit to the chapel.
1821 the City Assembly ordered that
he redundant bridge be removed but
his was never done, although the iron
ailings were later removed for conversion
nto munitions.

Roman Capping Stones

**Before you reach the canal locks
under the flyover, go up the
railed steps.** Fork left to see the
wall foundations. Here is a rebuilt
example of the Roman capping stones
or cornice and coping.

The unusual park suggests a Roman
amphitheatre but it was designed in
1996 and opened in 1997.

**Go through either arch in the
city wall and turn right.**

Steps to Morgan's Mount

**Climb steps onto the wall and
turn right. Proceed past the
rectangular tower.** Morgan's
Mount was named after a Captain
Morgan who, in the Civil War, had
a gun emplacement below the wall.

Go over the Northgate. The earlier
gate on this site contained the city

*Belltower of
the Bluecoat
Hospital*

gaol. In 1575 the shoe was on the
other foot when both city sheriffs
were locked up for not collecting
fines. A few years later, on 30th May
1578, the whole Company of Butchers
were imprisoned here for not supplying
enough meat for the city's needs and
forming a confederacy against country
butchers. To be incarcerated in the
airless, dark cells was not a pleasant
fate and they were released on the
13th June after their humble
submission was accepted by the
mayor. The 'drop' was first used here
for executions in 1801 but the gaol
was demolished in 1808 and prisoners
moved to the new gaol and House of
Correction on the site of the present
Queen's School. (See section 4.)

WALK

From page 60

Bridge of Sighs

Bluecoat Hospital

PH

NORTHGATE STREET

Northgate

ABBEY GREEN

Rufus Court

Canal

Deanery Field

Go to page 66

Turf Walls

Walls

King Charles' Tower

Roman stones

The Northgate (1810)

DURING demolition of the old Northgate, Thomas Harrison, the architect of the new gateway or bridge, discovered the remains of the Roman North Gate, the *Porta Decumana*.

LOOK TO YOUR LEFT to see the Victorian terracotta frontage of the Bull & Stirrup Hotel. Having the beast market in Upper Northgate Street led to pub names such as the White Bull, the Brown Cow and the Bull and Dog (now the Liverpool Arms).

Go down the steps onto Northgate Street. Go

LOOK FOR THE BLUE PLAQUE

through the arch if you want to see the front of the Bluecoat Hospital, built on a site formerly occupied by the Hospital of St John the Baptist, founded in the late 12th century for 'poor and sillie persons'. Records show that pensioners who were later housed here were given, 'a good loaf daily, a great dish of pottage, a piece of flesh or fish and a half-d -gallon of competant ale'.

LOOK FOR THE BLUE PLAQUE

Blue Boy Statue

The old hospital was knocked down to stop Parliamentary besiegers taking cover there during the Civil War. The new building of 1717 incorporated the Bluecoat School, the first charity scho built outside London by the Society for the Promotion of Christian Knowle The Bishop of Chester, Nicholas Strat was a signatory to the society's constitution in 1699 but the school was built ten years after his death. It was enlarged and rebuilt in 1854 when the life-sized 'blue boy' statue was incorporated into the new fron half of the central bay.

The SPCK still exists (although the school closed this century) and has a bookshop in St. Werburgh Street

Turn along Northgate Street towards the city centre but in only 25 metres turn left into Abbey Green and Rufus Court.

Turn immediately left through the entrance to the hidden courtyard. Rufus Court emulate the ancient galleried rows of Ches and won a design award when it was built in 1995.

62

Rufus Court

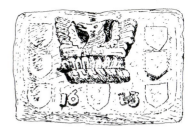

The phoenix on the tower

as access to houses in Abbey Green.

FURTHER ON is the Deanery Field. The banks inside the walls are the remains of first-century Roman turf walls. Carefully look over the wall to your left to see the bulge of the Roman wall below. Chester Coroners' records for 26th November 1719 record the unfortunate death of Ann Edge who wasn't so careful: she fell off the wall here by the Phoenix Tower. With a name like that perhaps it was inevitable.

Head up the iron spiral stairs, turn right and go up the narrow steps. Turn right onto the city wall. A small sandstone doorway above the car park was either built in 1662 as access to the bowling green built on the abbey orchard or in 1768

Illustration of 1895 H. Hovell Crickmore

The phoenix carving on the front of the corner tower is the emblem of the Painters, Glaziers, Embroiderers and Stationers Company who, in 1613, were given permission to repair the roof which was '*uncoered with leade and rayne discending upon and into the same.*'

This city guild held their meetings in the upper storey of the tower which was strewn with rushes and decorated with garlands of flowers at their annual meeting on the Festival of St Luke in October.

During the Civil War the guild met in Watergate Street while the tower was used for '*ordnance,*' probably a small gun emplacement. In 1645 King Charles I watched as his army was driven from Rowton Moor and fighting took place in the suburbs '*whence he removed to St Werburgh's steeple [the Cathedral tower] where, as he was talking with a captaine, a bullet from St John's gave him a salute*

WALK

A TALE OF

CIVIL WAR

SIR WILLIAM BRERETON was already unhappy with the city authorities who had tried to collect Ship Money for the King and murage for the city. Sir William had inherited Nunnes Hall within the walls but was a Cheshire MP not a Chester one. For a hundred years the city had been putting its own men in Parliament, one of whom was usually the Recorder.

Already with a puritanical streak, Brereton meant to fight for 'King and Parliament' if need be. The fact that the King had lost his senses and been persuaded by papists and traitors to stand against Parliament only made him harden his resolve.

Sir William and his men beat the drum at the cross to raise men and arms. It was the Mayor and his unholy brethren that caused the 'tumult' by putting the drum to the sword. Seeing his men imprisoned, himself exiled and his house burnt to the ground settled any doubts he still had.

Two weeks later Charles raised his banner at Nottingham. Nobody wanted to fight the King, only reform Parliament; but the die was cast.

The King visited Chester in September to receive his loyal gift - 100 pounds of gold. He had expected more.

Within a month or two the walls were repaired and outer defences dug from yet another tax on the citizens. Brereton was told of the Assembly order of 20th October: 'Three hundred inhabitants raised into an army and given muskets - eight men guarding each gate, night and day.'

Brereton's first attempt to take the city in July '43 failed due to lack of troops but with a feint attack on Boughton he managed to retire to the safety of the encampment at Tarvin.

Hawarden Castle, on the coast road, w captured in November but lost again in December by a sudden attack fr the city. A year went by with little movement on either side, then a heartening victory came to Brereton The Royalist army sent to reinforce Chester was defeated at Nantwich and, despite the city defences being strengthened, Brereton decided it was a good time to move in. Furth reinforcements in Chester and news another army marching north made him withdraw again but the troop were diverted to Naseby where the were sorely routed.

Men sent into Wales to find suppli brought back everything they could carry. News of pillage reached Lond Brereton was called to Parliament a only returned four months later. He almost laughed when he heard the results of attacks on Chester. The Mayor had escaped when the Parliam forces took the eastern suburbs b he left his dignity behind in the for of his sword and mace - and even h wife. Furthermore General Poyntz had devastated the King's troops outside the city.

The gun emplacement by St John's ha

reached the wall near the mured-up Newgate but it was a forlorn hope that the attackers would get through alive. When night came the city women patched up the breach with bedsteads.

Brereton sat, thought, wrote and planned. Both sides would soon be suffering from the winter. Both were more worried about food and supplies than fighting. His friends in the city reported that there was little meat left. They also told that the Lord St Paull, that French upstart, was found in bed with a minister's wife and Robert Grosvenor with 'another hore' at the Glovers' Stone.

Lord Byron was stubborn – he could have surrendered the city after the King left, but he held out until the end of January. The townspeople had to eat their dogs before he would give way. Byron himself had only boiled wheat and spring water for lunch.

A platform in St John's was to hold cannon atop the tower for the final assault but even supplies of block and tackle were short. No need now: Brereton's conditions for surrender were finally accepted, only a few aldermen refusing to sign. Sir William Brereton's forces marched through the open gates on 3rd February.

Despite surrender articles to the contrary, Brereton's soldiers took the city apart, smashing the High Cross and defacing the churches. The current Assembly and Mayor were discharged and new members elected. By April the Royalist army surrendered in England, with Harlech holding out for a further year in Wales.

By December 1648, attempts to reason with the King had failed. Colonel Pride's 'Purge' of Parliament denied 240 members but – as one of the trusted 'Rump' – Brereton was appointed to the Commission to try the King for treason.

Brereton had fought for 'Parliament and the King', always believing that Charles would have to concede to Parliament's demands. Could Parliament exist without a king? Could it exist with a king who was a 'man of blood'?

Charles refused to plead. Brereton never took his seat and never signed the Final Death Warrant. Charles was proclaimed a traitor nationwide – in Chester at the base of the High Cross. On 30th January 1649 the King was beheaded. Brereton died in Croydon a year after the Restoration of the Monarchy and the crowning of Charles II.

Cannon Emplacement

feature

From page 62

Canal

King Charles' Tower

Deanery Field

Roman stones

Turf Walls

Walls

ABBEY SQUARE

ABBEY ST

Kaleyard's Gate

slope

✝ 692 ft

Go to page 72

Cathedral

narrowly missing the king, hit the said captaine in the head, who died in the place.'

In 1854 a Mr Benjamin Huxley was allowed to rent the top floor at a rent of 2s6d per annum provided that he 'only use it as an observatory'.

The tower is now known as King Charles' Tower and houses a Civil War Exhibition.

Pass the wooden steps on your left and a stone set on your right. Just beyond the steps, at the top of the slope, look at the top of the wall to see the anchor mark and carving. It represents the length of the enormous Great Eastern

Length of the Great Eastern

launched in 1858. (The length is more than the distance from here to King Charles' Tower) The ship, originally known as the Leviathan, was built in four years by Isambard Kingdom Brunel and weighed 19,216 tonnes compared with the large ships of the day which

had a tonnage of a third of that. Willi Haswell, a master mason, and Mr Mus from the woodyard beside Cow Lane B were so impressed that they recorded the event here.

Go down the slope on your right. Do not go through the doorway.

Edward I granted the monks of Saint Werburgh's Abbey permission to have a gate in the city walls to reach their kale yard (vegetable garden).

Kaleyard's Gate

however, two gates were built which resulted in court wrangling between the Abbot and the Mayor. 'It was covenanted that the said abbot and convent and their successors should hold the postern closed in time of peace, on condition that they make a drawbridge across the ditch in the garden of the said abbey.' By the 16th century the larger gate had been walled up.

During the Civil War, Sir William Brereton, attacking the city for Parliament, reported that, 'All the Ports [gates] made up and strong guards sett upon them some of them within pistoll shott soe that none remained open but one little salley porte which is betwixt the Phenix Tower and the Eastgate.

THE CURFEW bell is still rung from 8.45pm. At 9pm each night, the Kaleyard's Gate is closed by a Cathedral verger. The Curfew, which was practised in many English cities, dates back to the Norman law of 'Couvrefeu' (coverfire) when fires had to be extinguished and citizens shut up safe inside their houses to protect the city at night. Even in the 18th century, street walking was frowned upon. A Chester diarist, Prescott, records that, on 18th November

1715, the 'Belman at the Cross near us Reads publicly a proclamacion in the Mayor's name, commanding all persons in the City to bee of peacable and civil behaviour, not to walk about the Streets or Rows at unreasonable Hours of the night.'

Carriageway and cobbles

Walk along the cobbled street behind the Cathedral. Look up on the walls of the Georgian houses, numbers 5 and 7, to see two small fire signs from the Sun Company. *See Feature on FireFighters.*

Fork left through Abbey Square with its paved carriageway.

TWO of four houses, built by Bishop Bridgeman in 1626, stand next to the rear entrance of the Cathedral. Here is a chance to visit, or just sample, the reasonably priced meals in the 14th-century refectory. Unlike the monks from Saint Werburgh's Abbey, you will not have to sit in silence whilst devotional words are spoken from the stone pulpit. The main visitor entrance is further along the walk.

LOOK FOR THE BLUE PLAQUE

House of 1626

WALK

The Benedictine Abbey of St.

TODAY'S Cathedral is on the site of Saint Werburgh's Abbey. This, in turn, is on the site of Saxon churches built on the rubble of the Roman fortress of DEVA.

It is said that St Peter's and St Paul's Church was founded here in around 660AD. Later, in the early tenth century, the remains of St Werburgh were brought to Chester from Staffordshire ostensibly to protect the holy relics from the marauding Danes.

The church was rededicated to St Werburgh while St Peter's was moved to its present position by the Cross. St Werburgh's became a Minster of secular priests under the Saxon Earl Leofric and his famous wife Lady Godiva.

The first Norman earl, Hugh, founded Saint Werburgh's Abbey for Benedictine Monks in 1092. Most of the abbey was built in just over a century. Then the monks started to knock down the abbey church and rebuild it in Gothic style. This amazing building programme lasted a total of 435 years.

Norman building work can be seen in the Baptisty, the North Transept, and the shop and exhibition centre of the present Cathedral.

SAINT WERBURGH'S SHRINE (c1310)

Saint Werburgh's Shrine was originally decorated with 34 Mercian princes and princesses. Werburgh was the daughter of Wulfere, King of Mercia (658-675). As a nun she was given control of all the Mercian nunneries.

A carved 'misericord' (monk's seat) in the quire shows three scenes from the legend of St Werburgh.

MISERICORDS (MONK'S SEATS)

Under the quire seats are ledges so that the monks could rest in a semi-standing position. In the late 14th century woodcarvers came from Lincoln to build the Tabernacled Stalls. Forty-three medieval scenes remain under the seats. After three years or so the woodcarvers moved on to Westminster Hall.

The Chester Imp

CHESTER IMP

Like Lincoln, Chester has its own imp. A stone carving on the north balcony of the Nave in the present cathedral is said to represent the Devil, bound hands and feet. It was apparently put there to frighten off the Devil if he should try to look through the window to see the sacrament.

Carved Bench End (c19th)

feature

Werburgh, Chester

BENCH ENDS

...any of the bench ends in the choir have ...urvived from the late 14ᵗʰ century. An elephant, ...oviously unknown to the carver, has horse's ...ooves. A pelican, symbol of piety, restores ...s young with blood from its own breast.

REFECTORY

...a pulpit in the refectory or monks' ...ining room ensured that they made ...ood use of their mealtimes.

GAMES

...n between prayers, work and meals the ...nonks could not have had much spare ...ime. However, a carving under the Northwest ...ower (now the Baptistry) suggests that, like ...nonks countrywide, they played Nine Men's Morris or Merels.

Carved Nine Men's Morris Board

FAIR

Each year the abbey received all the tolls of stalls set up in front of the abbey gate on Saint John the Baptist's Day.

Carved stone figure of the monk, Ranulph Higden, on the outside wall of the South Transept. His tomb is in the South Aisle of the Cathedral, the present Chapel of St Erasmus.

There is a stained-glass window, depicting Higden, in the Slype of the Cathedral.

Saint Werburgh's Shrine, with her relics, was said to have miraculous properties. In Saxon times, at the attack of King Gruffydd of Wales, her remains were carried to the top of the walls and 'struck the King blind' so that he retreated. On another occasion the shrine was carried in procession around the city to stop a great fire.

2am Matins followed by Lauds
6am (daybreak) Prime followed by Chapter Meeting
9am Terce   12am Sext   3pm None
6pm Vespers   7pm Compline

Within this tight schedule of services and devotion, Ranulph Higden, who entered the abbey in 1299 and died in 1363, wrote (or edited and collated) the Polychronicon. This seven volume history of the world was translated into English (from the original Latin) and printed in 1482. It was reprinted several times over the centuries.

Higden left an acrostic of his name in each initial word of the first seven chapters, 'Presentem Cronicam Conpilavit Frater Ranulphus Cestrensis Monachus'.

feature

THE DISSOLUTION of the Monasteries under Henry VIII saw the surrender of St Werburgh's Abbey on 20th January 1540. Ten monks were kept on for new duties in the cathedral including the abbot who became the dean. Eleven were pensioned off and seven others may have become priests or curates.

During the Autumn of 1538 many bargains had been struck with local gentry, who had managed to rent estates from the abbey for long periods for small sums. Because these leases were made a year before the surrender of the abbey, the contracts stood. Coincidentally it was the 'visitor' to the abbey, Dr Legh, who had signed a 99 year lease for two manors, and he had much to gain by postponing the abbey closure for 14 months or so.

The new cathedral was founded in August 1541. Little building work was done for several centuries and the building fell into disrepair. Major restoration was carried out in the 19th and 20th centuries; the most extensive work by Sir George Gilbert Scott between 1868 and 1876.

Key to plan

A Chapel of St Werburgh (Christian Unity)
B St Mary Magdalene Chapel (Children's Chapel)
C St Oswald's Chapel
D St George's Chapel (Cheshire Regt since 1912)
E St Nicholas and St Leonard's Chapel (Saints of children and pensioners)
F RAF Memorial Chapel
G Book of Names, Cheshire Regiment
H Chester Hearse Cloth
I Burial place of the Norman earls
J First Duke of Westminster Memorial
K HMS Chester Memorial
L Memorial to Thomas Green (Mayor 1565) and his wives. The hands may have been smashed by Puritans after the Civil War.
M Consistory Court 1636 (The only surviving in England)
N Apparitor's Chair
O Above is the Chapel of St Anselm (reserved for services)
P Font in the Baptistry
Q Nine Men's Morris Board carving
R Four mosaics of Old Testament scenes (1883-6)
S Thomas Brassey Bust
T Tomb said to be for Godescallus (Henry V of Aquitaine)
U Gurney radiator once used coke in the boiler
V Quire stalls include carved misericords, c1390
W Stained-glass Virgin & Child with six northern saints
X St John Ambulance & Red Cross Banner 1914-19
Y Sedile (clergy's seat) and Piscina (holy water basin)
Z Stone pulpit

α Stained-glass of St Werburg and her relation includes Shrine repelling Welsh invaders and Ethelred resigning Crown on Werburgh's advice
b Early English c1200 door to Refectory
c Recessed cupboards
d Monks' lavatorium (wash place)
e Stairs to Dorter (monks' dormitory) Conversion to purpose-built Song School
f Roof bosses include a 'green man' with foliage coming from his mouth
g Monks' vestment cupboard
h Later column blocks early doorway
i Overhead Bosses: Holy Trinity
   Our Lady and Child
   St Thomas Beckett's marty
j Carols (Monks' study areas)
k Burial places of early abbots
l Memorial to Bishop (1672-86) John Pearson
m Caterpillar web picture from Tyrol
n Remains of Norman quire
o Carved heads including Gladstone and D
p Monument of Bishop (1848-65) Graham
q Ranulph Higden's tomb and two others
r Quire screen (Gilbert Scott 1876)
s Chester Imp on the balcony
t Remains of fireplace
u C16th Cartoon tapestry - St Paul and Elymas
v Stained-glass of earls and King Henry VI
w Portions of old organ screen
x Stained-glass Ranulph Higden
y Stained-glass Saints and Apostles (1921-27)
z Saint Werburgh's Shrine (restored 1888)

feature

the blessed virgin mary ✝

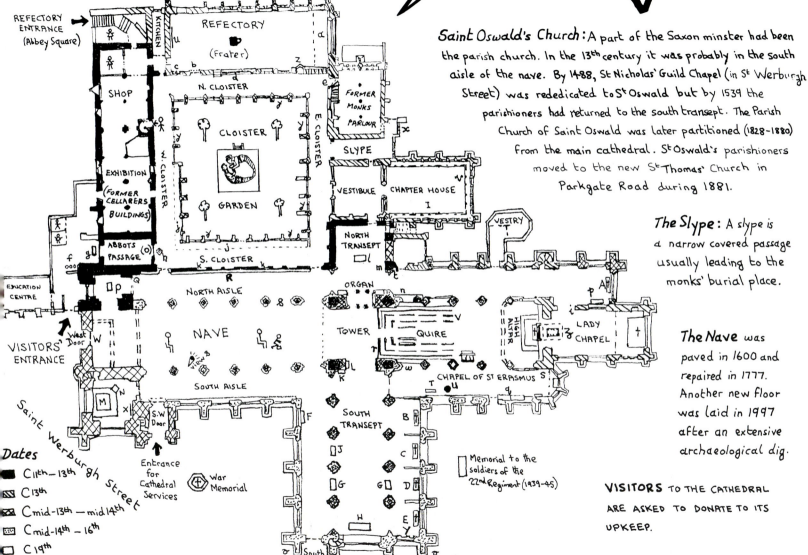

REFECTORY ENTRANCE (Abbey Square) →

KITCHEN

REFECTORY (Frater)

N. CLOISTER

SHOP

FORMER MONKS' PARLOUR

E. CLOISTER

CLOISTER GARDEN

W. CLOISTER

EXHIBITION (FORMER CELLARERS BUILDINGS)

SLYPE

VESTIBULE CHAPTER HOUSE

ABBOTS PASSAGE

S. CLOISTER

VESTRY

EDUCATION CENTRE

NORTH TRANSEPT

NORTH AISLE

ORGAN

VISITORS' ENTRANCE West Door

NAVE

TOWER QUIRE

LADY CHAPEL

SOUTH AISLE

CHAPEL OF ST ERASMUS

Saint Werburgh Street

S.W. Door

Entrance for Cathedral Services

War Memorial

SOUTH TRANSEPT

Memorial to the soldiers of the 22nd Regiment (1939-45)

South Door

Dates
- ■ C 11th–13th
- ▨ C 13th
- ▦ C mid-13th – mid 14th
- ▢ C mid-14th – 16th
- □ C 19th

feature

Saint Oswald's Church: A part of the Saxon minster had been the parish church. In the 13th century it was probably in the south aisle of the nave. By 1488, St Nicholas' Guild Chapel (in St Werburgh Street) was rededicated to St Oswald but by 1539 the parishioners had returned to the south transept. The Parish Church of Saint Oswald was later partitioned (1828-1880) from the main cathedral. St Oswald's parishioners moved to the new St Thomas' Church in Parkgate Road during 1881.

The Slype: A slype is a narrow covered passage usually leading to the monks' burial place.

The Nave was paved in 1600 and repaired in 1777. Another new floor was laid in 1997 after an extensive archaeological dig.

VISITORS TO THE CATHEDRAL ARE ASKED TO DONATE TO ITS UPKEEP.

Leave Abbey Square through the medieval Abbey Gateway. Look up to see the carved stone bosses under the vaulted roof.

Turn Left.

19th-century illustration of Abbey Gateway

The building (by Sir Arthur Blomfield in 1873) on your left was once the King's School, which was founded in 1541, after the Dissolution, by

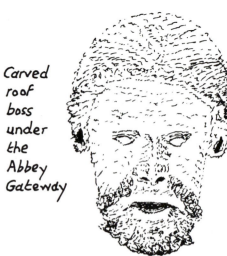

Carved roof boss under the Abbey Gateway

Henry VIII. Before that, the monks of the abbey would have taught local boys.

The Ravens' Nest →

Town Hall

Raven
Corvus corax

WALK

Saint Nicholas' Chapel

The Chapel of Saint Nicholas, built in 1280, was unacceptable to parishioners as a substitute to Saint Oswald's (then in the south aisle of the Abbey Church). As well as being used as the King's School in the 16th century, it became the Common Hall in 1545, the Wool Hall in 1727, the Theatre Royal in 1777, then the Music Hall in 1854. Later, in 1921, it became the oldest building in the world to be used as a cinema; closed in 1961.

Turn right along Music Hall Passage. Nearby is one end of Leen Lane, probably named after a Norman, Hugh de Leen.

Early English archway on S^t. Nicholas'

ne school was first held in the refectory any available part of the Cathedral well as in Saint Nicholas' Chapel, on Werburgh Street. The present King's hool is a mile south of the city.

rn **left into St Werburgh Street.** ere is another chance to visit the athedral, this time by the main sitor entrance.

ross over the road, walk along t Werburgh Row and pass the andstone building.

LOOK FOR THE BLUE PLAQUE

Music Hall Passage

Turn left at the street and, beyond three shops, turn left into Leen Lane and immediately right onto the row, once known as 'Broken Shin Row' because of the poor state of its surface. Beside the first set of steps look at the shop front on number 8 – the wooden shutters put up at night are some of the oldest in the city, only the shop name has changed. Until recently it belonged to a cheese wholesaler, a reminder of the 'butter shops and milkstoopes' here since medieval times.

Go down the first set of steps. Above you the drainpipe from the same shop is probably the oldest in the city: it may date from 1740.
Around the corner is the Cross.

WALK

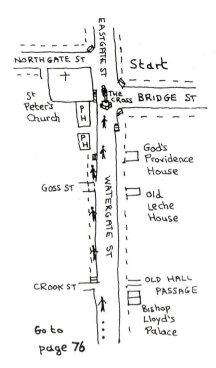

THE WALK

SECTION 4   2·5 Km

Old Port & Canal

NORTHWEST QUARTER OF CHESTER

FROM THE CROSS, head down Watergate Street for about 45 metres.

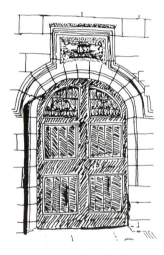

An old door on Watergate Street

LOOK up to your left to see God's Providence House. In legend, the owner, whose family had survived the plague, had the religious motto 'God's providence is mine inheritance' put up on the house which was built or rebuilt in

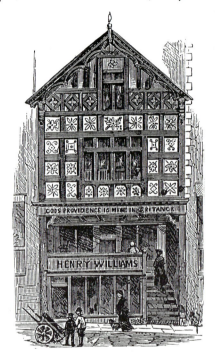

C19th engraving of God's Providence House

1652. (It has been rebuilt since then.) Other Chester houses have similar religious mottos and the same words can be found on other houses in this country. The plague or Black Death hit Chester hard in the 17th century. From a total population of less than 7,000, 1313 people died of this insidious disease in 1605 whilst in 1647, shortly after the chaos and starvation of the Civil War, a further 2,032 people died in 23 weeks.

The street leads to the Watergate

WALK

74

the 16th century many rich merchants
inhabited this street which led down
to the Watergate and the port on
the River Dee. The cellars or vaults,
partly below street level, were used
as warehouses and shops. On the
left are several of these dating from
the 13th, or possibly 12th, century. These
may have stood on Roman foundations
cut into the sandstone bedrock.
Nowadays the street is known for its
antique shops.

Climb the steps on your right and
turn left. The first floor gallery, sometimes including the 'cellars' below, was
called 'le flessherowe', a butchers' row
existing by 1345 and also recorded
in 1545. Later on, butchers had a
'shambles' (tables used by meat vendors)
in Northgate Street.

Continue along the row. Further
along look across at the front of Leche
House (see Section 1) decorated with
vines and grapes.

At the end of the row descend the
steps and continue down Watergate
Street. Look left again to see the
richly decorated Bishop Lloyd's Palace.
The western half of the house, originally
built in 1615, supports biblical scenes

Bishop Lloyd's Palace, 1826 engraving by George Cuitt

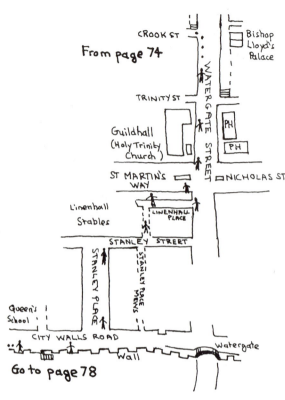

From page 74

CROOK ST

Bishop Lloyd's Palace

WATERGATE STREET

TRINITY ST

Guildhall (Holy Trinity Church)

PH

PH

ST MARTIN'S WAY

NICHOLAS ST

Linenhall Stables

LINENHALL PLACE

STANLEY STREET

STANLEY PLACE

STANLEY PLACE MEWS

Queen's School

CITY WALLS ROAD

Wall

Watergate

Go to page 78

The SS Rosabelle

Sketch by B. Emery

such as Adam and Eve, Cain and Abel, and Abraham about to sacrifice his son Isaac. Before the bishop came to Chester, his bishopric was Sodor and Man: hence the 'Legs of Man' next to his family crest of three horses' heads. Formerly two houses, in 1666 Lady Kilmorey bought the western one for £450 and the dilapidated eastern one for £44. She then joined them together. They have been rebuilt since.

THE GUILDHALL on your right has a museum open Thursday, and Saturday morning, telling the history of Chester's important trade guilds who monopolised the local economy for centuries. All councillors, aldermen, sheriffs and mayors had to be elected from their ranks.

LOOK FOR THE BLUE PLAQUE

OPPOSITE the pub of the same name is the Old Custom (&Excise) House, situated between the port and the city. In 1810 the Magna Britannia reported that there were 'more ships built at Chester than at Liverpool' and, as late as the 1880s, square-rigged schooners, barquentines and sailing barges were still sailing up to Crane Wharf. Steam coasters such as the 'Rosabelle' still used the port until the 1930s.

The Old Custom House

Cross St Martin's Way at the ligh then turn right into Linenhall Pla

Thomas Pennant in 'The Journey from Chester to London' related that 'In Ma 1780, I began my annual journey to Londo At Chester some improvements had taken place since my last account of the ci A very commodius building had been erected in the Yachtfield near the Watergate street for the sale of Irish Linen at the two fairs. It surrounds a large square area; on each side of which are piazzas, with numbers of sh well adapted for the purpose'.

he Yachtfield (possibly named after the acht pub that lay on the course of the resent dual carriageway) was, in turn, n the site of the Grey Friars' Monastery. When the Linen Hall was removed to make way for the current stables, rchaeologists dug glazed tiles from he underlying ruins.

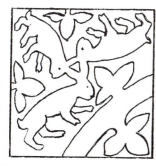

A tile from Grey Friars Monastery

At the end of the cul-de-sac, turn left at the stables, down the alley. At the road, cross to the pavement, turn right, then left down Stanley Place. Bootscrapers stand outside almost every door.

Cross to the city walls and turn right to follow them. Pass the decorated Victorian terracotta frontage of the Queen's School, founded 1878 and opened in 1883. The House of Correction and the City Gaol once stood on the site.

The Statue of Queen Victoria on the Queen's School.

Queen Victoria statues can also be found outside the Queen Hotel, in the Castle yard, and in St Werburgh Street.

Terracotta Chimney

The Infirmary, further on, first opened in the Bluecoat Hospital outside the North- gate in 1756 but moved here five years later. It was one of the first hospitals in the country to have isolation wards for infectious diseases. Chester's modern hospital 'The Countess of Chester' is on the Liverpool Road, a mile from the city.

Chester Quay (old engraving)

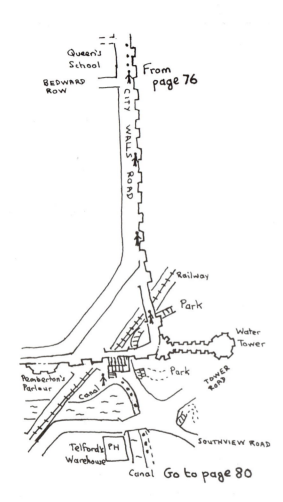

Queen's School

BEDWARD ROW

CITY WALLS ROAD

From page 76

Railway

Park

Water Tower

Pemberton's Parlour

Canal

Park

TOWER ROAD

Telford's Warehouse PH

SOUTHVIEW ROAD

Canal Go to page 80

Continue along the walls over the railway bridge. In 1845 the Chester & Holyhead Railway works began by felling trees here. Trains had already reached Chester. The first, in 1840, was the steam engine 'Wirral' pulling ten carriages.

Bonewaldesthorne's Tower and the Water Tower (Engraved before the railwa...

tower, and is well worthy of notice. We can promise the reader very great gratification and amusement from this excellent instrument which will furnish him with a most charming prospect of the diversified and lovely scenery which

The strangely-named Bonewaldesthorne's Tower beside the wall is topped by a camera obscura: a single convex lens above the roof projects images onto a white round table in the darkened upper room. Roberts' Chester Guide of 1851 mentions an earlier model 'which is situated on the upper part of the

nature has so profusely spread around. The beautiful view of the winding Dee and the picturesque country on its banks is most delightful, and cannot fail to excite very pleasurable emotion... Unfortunately some of the view has been obscured in the name of progress, and the tower, at the time of writing, is closed

THE WATER TOWER stands out in the park. William the Conqueror's Domesday Book of 1086 records that, before the conquest, 'if ships arrived or departed from the port of the city without the king's licence, the king and earl had 40 shillings from each man who was on the ships. If the king's reeve ordered those who had marten pelts not to sell to anyone until they had first been shown to him and he had bought, whoever neglected this paid a fine of 40 shillings'

Chester's port was still flourishing in 1195 when a local monk, Lucian, wrote: 'Chester has, beneath its walls, a beautiful river abounding with fish, with a harbour on its south side where ships from Aquitaine, Spain, Ireland and Germany unload their cargoes of wine and other merchandise.' In fact, wine was only imported through five English ports: London, Sandwich, Southampton, Bristol and Chester.

By 1322, the river was silting up and moving away from the west wall so that John Helpstone was employed at a cost of £100 (perhaps worth £100,000 today) to build a port watch tower (the Water Tower).

The River Dee Basin entrance to the Chester Canal (old engraving)

After the Dissolution of the Monasteries, under Henry VIII, the 'curiously wrought ornamental spire' of White Friars Monastery (see section 1) was kept until 1597 as an aid to navigation on the Dee which, at that time, was treacherous with moving sands. It is said that part of the English/Welsh border,

only a mile from the city (now in the centre of the new Chester football ground) was formed after a ship hit a sandbank in the middle of the river. The Cheshire people of England refused to help with the bodies of the sailors but the parishioners of Hawarden in Wales gave them decent burials. Later, when the river was canalised in the 'new cut', allowed by Act of Parliament in 1732, Hawarden claimed the boundary to where the sandbank had been.

The new cut was supposed to increase shipping trade by making one deep channel through to the Dee Estuary, but the canalised river never reached its proposed depth of 16 feet (5 metres). Ships grew larger and, boosted by its profits from the slave trade, so did the Port of Liverpool, leaving Chester to become a backwater.

Go down the next steps on the left.

WALK

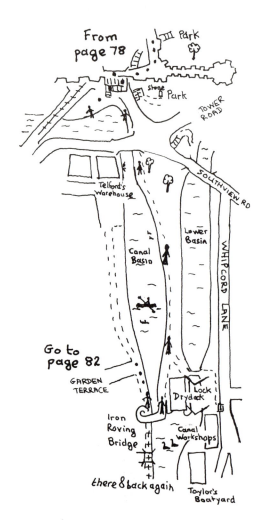

From page 78

Park

Stone Park

TOWER ROAD

SOUTHVIEW RD

Telford's warehouse

Canal Basin

Lower Basin

WHIPCORD LANE

Go to page 82

GARDEN TERRACE

Iron Roving Bridge

Lock Drydock

Canal Workshops

there & back again

Taylor's Boatyard

Having taken the steps down from the walls, look to your left. The bluish stone in the park below the Water Tower may be the original Glovers' Stone, a marble-like boundary stone which once stood between the city limits and the Castle. *See Castle feature.*

Fork right to the canalside.

After looking at the ropemarks left by horse-drawn barges on the corner of the railway bridge turn **left** along the towpath.

Originally the Chester Canal carried straight on to the river here, but in 1795 the Wirral Arm of the Ellesmere Canal [to Whitby Wharf (now Ellesmere Port) on the Mersey] joined it and the layout was altered, creating a sharp bend. Look for the iron ring and hook. Without it, barges towed by horses would have crashed into the far wall when turning the bend.

Metal post protecting stone bridge

Ring & Hook

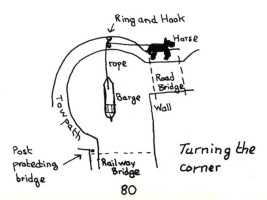

Ring and Hook

Horse

rope

Road Bridge

Barge

Towpath

Wall

Post protecting bridge

Railway Bridge

Turning the corner

ON the canal edge grows a nettle lookalike called gypsywort. It received its name after being used by fortune tellers to darken their skin and appear as gypsies. In 1562 an Act of Parliament was passed that ma[de] it illegal for anyone to cons[ort] with 'Egyptian[s]' or counterfeit[ing] their speech or behaviour.

Gypsywort

Water Dock

CROSS the canal is the loading bay of Telford's Warehouse. An impressive water dock grows beside the wall.

Fork right at the drydock. Boatowners can hire this 'Graving Dock', built in 1798, for repairs. Two full length (16·46 metres) narrowboats can fit in. The flat-bottomed canal boats rest on large sleepers giving access to the underneath. Narrowboats were traditionally made with freshly cut elm planks 10cm thick on the

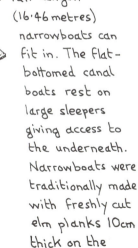

Sluice gear

bottom. The sides of these working boats were normally 5cm oak planks with 2·5cm internal shearing. The fresh elm bottoms always stayed wet and did not need treating but the sides were tarred with a mixture of coal tar and pitch. Some 'dayboats' which could have a rudder at either end to save turning round, just used pine for the side planks as they were

The Canal Basin 1998

built for a shorter lifespan. All the boats had their seams 'caulked' (packed) with 'oakum' (combed fibre) to make them watertight.

TAYLOR'S boatyard, beyond the drydock, originally was run by the Canal company, but after the Shropshire Union sold off its fleet, it was rented by a family boatbuilding firm. Many of the wooden River Dee pleasure boats were built here and each year return to the

Roving Bridge

dock for overhaul.

ALONGSIDE the drydock is a lock to the Lower Basin. In emergency the lock can be converted to another drydock.

Cross the 'roving bridge' over the canal. Imagine a horse with a towrope attached to a barge, to understand the principle behind the contorted passage of the towpath over this bridge. The ropemarks on the beginning of the iron railing must have been made only as boats proceeded towards the city.

Moorhen
Gallinula
chloropus

WALK

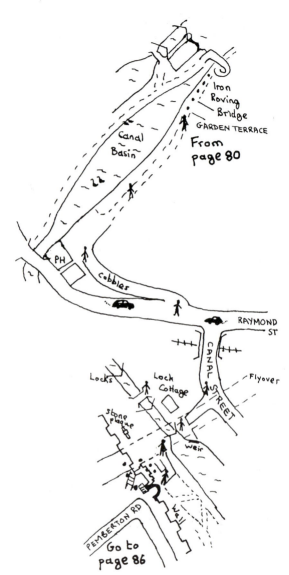

From page 80

Iron Roving Bridge

GARDEN TERRACE

Canal Basin

PH

cobbles

RAYMOND ST

CANAL STREET

Flyover

Locks

Lock Cottage

stone plaque

weir

PEMBERTON RD

Go to page 86

there and back again

The towpath leads out past the Countess of Chester Hospital, under George Stephenson's eleven arch railway viaduct of 1840, and into the countryside. Wander as far as you like (it is 10 miles for the hardened walker or canal enthusiast to reach the Ellesmere Port Boat Museum), returning here to continue the route.

Stay on this bank and walk towards Chester, passing Telford's Warehouse.

Thomas Telford

Thomas Telford was the General Agent, Surveyor, Engineer, Architect and Overlooker of the Works on the Ellesmere Canal for a salary of £300 per annum under William Jessop, the Chief Engineer. Soon, Telford's proficiency, particularly with the famous iron aqueduct at Pontcysyllte near Llangollen, had him promoted.

INSIDE the warehouse, now a popular pub, the iron crane to lower goods to boats below still exists.

THE ORIGINAL canalside pub here was the Ellesmere Canal Tavern once situated next door. Shortly after the canal opened, a packet boat to Liverpool ran from here. The boat, pulled by two horses, could reach speeds of 10-12 miles per hour creating only a small bow wave (much faster than an engine driven boat which would create drag and a rear wash in the narrow canal). This meant that the passengers could, for 1s 6d = 1st Class or 1s = 2nd Class, reach Liverpool in three hours, using the Countess of Bridgewater Steamboat to cross the Mersey. This speedy and comfortable journey, compared to coach travel on bumpy roads, made shopping in Liverpool all the fashion.

Needless to say, the Ellesmere Canal Tavern did a roaring trade with the passing custom.

ELLESMERE CANAL TAVERN.
CHESTER.

J. Ackerley Captain of the
Canal Packet.

Respectfully informs the Ladies
Gentlemen travelling betwixt
Liverpool & Chester that Breakfast,
Dinner, Tea & every requisite
accommodation may be had in the
Packet which sails daily betwixt
these Places, he has likewise fitted
up the above Tavern with good
Beds, Wines, Spirituously malt Liquors
for the entertainment of Families,
Travellers & the public in general
whose Favors he humbly solicits
assuring them it will be his
constant study to merit their
Approbation and support.

Copy of an advertisement for the 'Packet'

Turn left up the cobbles. Carefully cross the main road. Turn left then right into Canal Street. At the first bend take the entry to the canal under the flyover. Cross the bridge over the canal locks.

Five ages of transportation.
Chester Canal 1772. First Chester balloon 1785
First train to Chester 1840
Chester Buses from 1930
Beyond is Hawarden Airport

There were originally five locks on the Chester Canal cut into sandstone and heading straight down to the river. It was only when the Wirral Arm was installed that they were reduced to three

Inside the locks are ladders in case boatmen or 'gongoozlers'* fall in.

On the horizon is Moel Famau (Welsh for 'mothers' mountain') The nipple shape on the top of the mountain is not the reason for the name (which is said to come from the mother goddesses of Celtic mythology). Rather it is the remains of George III's Jubilee Tower which was designed by Thomas Harrison but fell down only a few years later.

Turn left along the towpath but immediately beyond the flyover take the cobbled slope up.

At the corner carefully look over to the towpath below. A board set into the path covers a set of steps - this was for canal horses to climb in case they fell in.

Turn right before the arch in the city wall.

*There are always plenty of gongoozlers around the locks in summer. The word is boatman's slang for those who stand and watch, without working!

WALK

THE CHESTER CANAL BEGUN 1772

Nantwich was completed in 1805, the same year the Montgomery Canal Lin[e] reached the Severn. The Chester Canal Company, buoyed by new business, merged with the Ellesmere Canal Company on 1st July 1813. Junctions we[re] made at Middlewich with the Trent and Mersey Canal in 1827, and [at] Nantwich to the Birmingham and Liverpool Canal in 1835. Business bo[omed]

However, by 1846 the railways played a large part in forward plannin[g] and the canal became part of the Shropshire Union Railways and Can[al] Company only to be leased to London & North Western Railways a year la[ter]

'President'. An early 20th century steam narrowboat from the fleet of Fellows, Moreton & Clayton Ltd.

Competition with Great Western Railw[ay] in this part of the country kept the canal system viable and the company ran its own boats until 1921 when 'economic conditions' made it 'impossible to continue'. Boats, horses and equipment were sold although th[e] canal was kept open for private traders. The followin[g] year the 'Shroppie' became a legal part of L&NWR, which in turn became part of London, Midland and Scottish Railways. Finally the canals were nationali[sed]. Nowadays the British Waterways (Board), established 1963, undertakes the maintenance of the canal.

THE FIRST sod from the Chester Canal was cut by the Mayor on 18th May 1772 and, in the belief that this was a new era of wealth and trade for the city, 21 guns fired a salute and bells were rung. The plan was to cut from the River Dee to Middlewich but difficulties led to the route ending at Nantwich. By 1780 the canal proved to be uneconomic and by 1787 it was virtually unusable. No doubt it would have been closed if the Ellesmere Canal Co. had not been formed. This company had the object of joining a canal to the rivers Mersey, Dee and Severn. The first section, which promised to give a good return for investment, was between Chester and Liverpool (ending at Whitby Wharf – now Ellesmere Port – on the Mersey). Cut by 1795 this Wirral Arm was immediately used by packetboats and coal 'flats', with trade increasing over the years. A direct line south from the Dee at Chester to Pontcysyllte Aqueduct near Llangollen was abandoned; the alternative junction to the Chester Canal at

Snowy, in towing regalia, pulled boats here until 1990. A children's book about her was published in 1992.

feature

CHESTER ROWS

By 1673 'all benches and showboards in the rows' had to be 'made with hinges' so they could be 'folded up at night'.

In the early 18th century, Daniel Defoe, thought the rows 'old and ugly' but Wesley in 1752 found them 'the greatest convenience,' especially in the rain.

Traders have never had it better. Where else in the world can you find four or five rows of shops in every street? There were once far more rows than those that remain. They stretched up Northgate Street, along Foregate Street and down Lower Bridge Street where a few portions still remain.

Certainly no walk or shopping trip in Chester would be the same without a stroll along the ancient rows.

CHESTER'S unique shopping galleries 'rows' have been recorded from the early 14th century. The first ones were probably built after a fire ravaged the city in 1278. Edward I was using Chester as a base in his wars against the Welsh and a large number of craftsmen came here from all over the country. The King's master craftsman, Richard Enginour (the engineer) settled here and became mayor of the city in 1305.

The medieval rows were very different from those that remain. Steps or ladders led to the first floor where narrow walkways made their way between shops and houses. These were often built upon stalls that leaned out from the stone vaults and timber-framed buildings below. If you could make your way along the creaky boards from one shop to another you would have to dodge displays of goods on the floor, walls, and hanging from the rafters; while stalls on the outside of the galleries dimmed the light.

Both the linencloth market and the cornmarket were once held in the rows, leaving traders to complain that the resulting obstructions stopped 'their' customers getting to 'their' shops.

In the evenings, gangs of ruffians would gather in these dark lofts and wait, perhaps for a chance to cut a purse free from its owner.

Boots hanging in Shoemakers' Row Northgate St. (Demolished)

feature

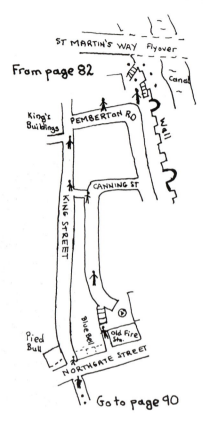

From page 82

St Martin's Way Flyover

Canal

King's Buildings

PEMBERTON RD

Wall

CANNING ST

KING STREET

Pied Bull

Blue Bell

Old Fire Stn.

NORTHGATE STREET

Go to page 90

Go through the gap by the ringroad to see the plaque marking the corner of the Roman wall.

Turn left, go under the steps, then first right along Pemberton Road. Ahead of you are King's Buildings.

LOOK FOR THE BLUE PLAQUE

Turn left.

King Street

86

Diagonally opposite the Chester Town House, go through the archway beside number 28.

Go along the alley then turn right.

At the end of the cul-de-sac climb the steps to Firemans Cottages.

Look to your left for the Golden Falc mosaic. Centurion House is on the site of this famous Chester hostelry, which became the Northgate Brewery.

Streetlight

Going towards Firemans Cottages

Clay pipe bowl found in a King Street garden

WALK

Golden Falcon mosaic

...ndel stayed here while he waited for the ...at to Ireland where he was to give the ...rst public performance of The Messiah. ...e arranged to practise some verses of ...e Messiah with members of the cathedral ...hoir but had some trouble with a local ...rinter who was a chorister. After ...rranging to have singers who could ...ead music, Handel found that the man ...as consistently out of tune. He cried ...ut in broken English, "You schauntrel, ...id not you tell me that you could ...ng at sight". ..."Yes Sir", said the printer, "and so I can, ...ut not at first sight"!

At the street turn right, after ...ooking up to see the interesting frontage of the old fire station of 1911. *See feature on Firefighters.*

Go under the arch of the Blue Bell and the Pied Bull.

The Bluebell is Chester's sole surviving medieval inn. Inside, a braced kingpost roof dates from the 15th century although parts of the building may date from the 11th century. The date 'licensed 1494' refers to the first type of pub licencing created by an Act of Parliament. Justices of the Peace were empowered to 'put away common ale selling where they should think convenient.'

In 1540 the inn was just called 'The Bell,' a well-used English pub name near churches.

The Blue Bell

Early records show 'William Bird of Yᵉ Bell Innholder' was admitted to the Innkeepers Guild in 1596.

Cross the main street. Now look back

at the Blue Bell. The roadside cabin was used as a ticket office for coaches, the small upstairs window to reach the coachmen and passengers sitting on deck with the baggage.

The first London-Chester Coach ran in 1657. By 1784 the landlord of the Pied Bull, John Paul, was running a coach to Birkenhead for ferries to Liverpool. Three years later John Paul moved his business to the White Lion, then in the Town Hall Square which was already taking the London Post Coach for six passengers. In 1818 a Mr G Steele saw the stone milepost outside the White Lion It said 'London 182 miles.'

TO
LONDON
198 MILES
WORCESTER
85 MILES
LUDLOW
68 MILES
BRISTOL
180 MILES
AND
BATH
185 MILES

OLD COACHING SIGN 1763

In 1675 John Ogilby recorded the distance to London as 182 miles, 1 furlong.

WALK

FIREFIGHTERS

Morris 85' Turntable Ladder 1938

1086 The Domesday Book records that if a fire burnt the city the person responsible was fined three pence and had to pay his neighbour two shillings.

1140 Fire destroys a large part of the city. (York was virtually destroyed in the same century, as were London and Carlisle in the 13th century.)

1180 A great fire is prevented by parading Saint Werburgh's Shrine through the streets.

1278 Another great fire sweeps the city.

1494 A great fire destroys much of Northgate Street.

1564 & 1565 Fires destroy Northgate Street and Handbridge.

1569 Chester Assembly orders 'for the better savegarde of the said citie from danger of ffyer...before Easter...every Alderman... shall have in redines four buckets... and every common counsaile... one buckett'

1591 A hook with rings (for pulling down buildings) is added to the city's fire equipment.

1709 The first volunteer fire brigade is formed and a fire engine house built for five hand-operated pumps. Despite a petition from the Bakers they are not allowed to stack more than 30 kids of gorse or faggots (bundles of sticks) in any building. Flaxdressers and Ostlers are banned from smoking at work or using open candles. No-one is allowed to store over 2lbs of gunpowder.

1761 A new fire engine house is built.

1762 Thirty firemen live within the city.

1803 The police force act as the fire brigade.

1846 A fire station is built in Northgate Street.

1853 The firemen/policemen resign (as firemen) as the work is too onerous.

Northgate Stree
Fire Station
1911

feature

Firemark or Fire Sign issued by the Sun Assurance Company.

This one is in Handbridge.

...in case any person or persons shall throw, disperse, or set fire to any Squibs, Rockets, Serpents, Crackers, or other Fire Works, or shall fire off any Gun or Pistol, expend and set fire to, or cause to be fired, any Gunpowder alone, or with any other Ingredient, or shall make or assist at the making of any openfire, usually called Bonfires or shall throw, disperse, or carry about any openfire, in any of the Streets, Lanes, Rows, Passages, or other Places within the said City... for every such seperate Offence the Sum of Ten Shillings, to be levied...

Excerpt from Improvement Act 1761

1862 The Exchange (town hall and market) burns down.

1863 The City of Chester Volunteer Fire Brigade is formed. The roll includes seven officers and sixty men. Any member heard to curse, swear or use any blasphemous expression on drill or duty is fined 5 shillings.

1870 A new fire engine house is built at the Potato Market in Northgate Street to house a horse-drawn manual engine, a wheeled ladder and a hand-drawn manual engine.

1895 Merryweather horse-drawn steam fire engine bought.

1911 Northgate Street Fire Station costing £3000 opens.

1914 A Morris-Belsize fire engine bought. The service becomes the City of Chester Fire Brigade. Sergeants paid 2 shillings for the first hour of the shift and a shilling thereafter.

1920, 1929, 1934, 1939 Dennis Brothers' fire engines are bought.

1938 Morris turntable ladder is bought.

1940 Fireman C G Dutton (Chester's first civilian war casualty) is killed by falling timbers after the 20th November air raid.

1941 The Fire Service is nationalised.

1948 The brigade reforms as City of Chester Fire Services.

1971 The new St Anne Street Fire Station opens.

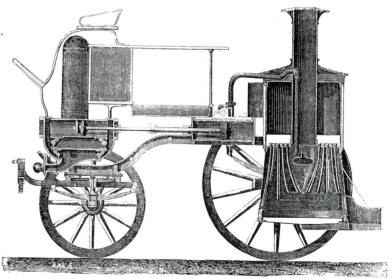

LONGITUDINAL SECTION OF MERRYWEATHER'S FIRE-ENGINE, AWARDED GOLD MEDAL AT THE PARIS INTERNATIONAL EXHIBITION, 1867.

Chester bought a 'Merryweather' in 1895

feature

From page 86

BlueBell
PH

KING
STREET
Pied
Bull

Odeon

HUNTER
STREET

Library

PH

PRINCESS
STREET

Town
Hall

Forum

Roman
Strongroom
HAMILTON
PLACE
PH

NORTHGATE STREET

cobbles

car
park

Little
Abbey
Gateway

Abbey
Square

Abbey Gateway

ST WERBURGH
STREET

MUSIC
HALL
PASSAGE

Go to page 94

Go down the cobbles opposite King Street, towards the car park. At the foot of the slope, turn right along the cobbled alley. This may have been the medieval 'Bell Lane linge between the house of the said Hugh [Alderseye] and the monasterie of sainte Werburge'. Most of the foundations of buildings here, within the old abbey grounds, are sandstone, suggesting that earlier stone foundations may have been used or reused. Brick was only in regular use after the late 16th century.

Two Listed Buildings

The medieval Little Abbey Gateway and the 'Art Nouveau' Odeon of 1936

Turn right again to exit via the Little Abbey Gateway opposite the Odeon Cinema. At the surrender of St Werburgh's Abbey in 1540, it had a brewhouse, a storehouse, a bakehouse with two ovens, the great kiln and the drying floor situated on the left of this alley.

Turn left, then cross over to pass the Westminster Coach & Motor Car Works, now the public library.

LOOK FOR THE BLUE PLAQUE

The Public Library

The city's first public library opened in 1773 in White Friars. Members were charged an annual subscription of a guinea (£1/1s/- or £1-05). A free public library was built in 1877 in St John Street. The present library opened in 1984.

WALK

E Westminster Works of J.A. Lawson & Co. ach Builders, Harness Makers and Motor gineers' was formed in 1902 but had ased trading here by 1914 leaving e terracotta frontage.

o past the Roman column bases display, and the Town Hall. **LOOK FOR THE BLUE PLAQUE**

WENTY-FIVE metres beyond the Forum trance look through the archway on ur right, signed 'To Hamilton Place' d 'To Chester Gateway Theatre' to see

the Roman strongroom, found when the market was rebuilt in 1967. Much of the Roman fortress of DEVA is still under Chester's buildings which follow the same main street pattern. Return through the arch (the only part of the old market hall still standing) to Northgate Street.

Continue down Northgate Street.

A Celebration of Chester by S Broadbent.

Stephen Broadbent, who also designed the holistic Water of Life sculpture in the Cathedral's cloister gardens, had his 'Celebration of Chester' unveiled by Lord Mayor, Councillor John Randall on 21st September 1992. It was commissioned by Chester City Council, The Dean of Chester Cathedral and the Capital Bank. The controversial sculpture represents thanksgiving, protection and industry.

Roman column bases, Roman drain and an 18th century column

The Old Market Hall Archway

WALK

THE ROMAN FORTRESS DEVA

A Roman Legionary

BUILT by the II Legion Adiutrix Pia Fidelis (loyal and true) on a rocky outcrop at the mouth of the sacred Celtic River Dyfrdwy, DEVA was on the former territory of the Cornovii. The site was ideal as a western port to import supplies, export lead and slaves, and attack Ierne (Ireland).

When the XX Legion Valeria Victrix (brave and victorious) took over the fortress they began to rebuild it in stone. However, only twenty years later, the legion marched north to build the momentous wall for Emperor Hadrianus. By 163A wall building in Scotland was abandoned and the XX Legion returned to reoccupy and rebuild DEVA. Outside the walls a civilian settlement developed to supply labour, goods and women for the vast force of soldiers assembled here from all over the Continent. Outside the walls, also, cemeteries lined the Roman roads with highly coloured carvings and inscriptions. Temples to the gods were set up to ensure the soldiers' good fortune.

A giant palace 'praetorium' for the Legate stood opposite the huge columns of the legionary headquarters 'principia'. Barracks lined the north and south walls. Granaries and stores were kept within the fortifications.

Antefix (roof tile) of the 20th Legion 'Valeria Victrix' deployed at DEVA (Chester) from AD 86 to about AD 287.

LEG XX

OTH inside and outside the walls were bath-houses
'ermae'. Here the men could think of warmer climes
they relaxed in the hot water and chatted to their
ends about the sport in the amphitheatre and news
the empire.

eek doctors employed in the fort practised their life-
pporting arts and erected altars to Asclepius, Hygeia
d Panakeia, but it was the Roman gods and
ddesses who received the most favour. Altars and
rines to Jupiter, Fortuna, Nemesis, Minerva and gods
the household and legion stood in the buildings.
e boar, symbol of the XX Legion faced the tiled
ofs. Many were left or buried when the legions
parted to Gaul (France) along with hoards of silver
d other riches too heavy or dangerous to carry, some
t discovered to this day.

A mythical beast with a scarlet
eye in a green enamel body is
a unique example of Romano-
British art on a seal box lid
(used to hold wax impressions)
found under the present Odeon
cinema.

Copper
AS coin
of the
Emperor
Hadrian
AD 117-138

PLAN OF
DEVA
Key

I Principia (HQ) II Praetorium (Legate's Palace)
III Centuriae (Legionary Barracks) IV Auxilia (Auxiliary Barracks)
V Scamnum Tribunorum (Tribunes' Houses) VI Horrea (Granaries)
VII Valetudinaria (Hospital Buildings) VIII Fabrica (Workshops)
IX Thermae (Baths) X Circus (Amphitheatre)

feature

From page 90

Forum

Roman
Strongroom

PH

NORTHGATE STREET

MUSIC
HALL
PASSAGE

LEEN
LANE

PH

at
Commercial
Newsrooms

Ye Olde
Deva

PH

PH

St Peter's Church

WATERGATE
STREET

THE
CROSS

EASTGATE ST.

BRIDGE
ST

LETTERS

POST   OFFICE

Replica Victorian
Post Box outside
the Town Hall

After noting the city's motto and the statues on the black and white corner building, proceed along the raised 'row' ahead. Either this or a row opposite was known, in 1330, as 'Iurnemongerrowe de Nortgate strete'. On 23rd August 1616, King James I walked along

demolished at the end of the 19th centur

As the row drops you reach th old Commercial Newsrooms.

LOOK FOR THE BLUE PLAQUE

Turn right up the passage into St Peter's Churchyard. In November 1636, complaint was made

Late 19th century engraving of Shoemakers' Row, Northgate Street

'Shoemakers' Row' on this side of the street on his way from the cathedral to a banquet at the Pentice alongside St Peter's Church. Shoemakers' Row was

that ' the way is used thorow the Church and Church-yard to the said three doors going to the said three houses next adjoining to drink Wyne

The Former Commercial Newsrooms

eer and ale upon Sundays, holidayes
nd other days. And divers p'rsons goe
horowe the said church-yard to the
aid severall tap houses at there (sic)
leasure to drinke makinge the Church
ard a mere passage...'. They still do!

urn left into the yard and then
iagonally right onto another
assage. When you emerge onto
Watergate Street North Row,
urn left. The site of Ye Olde Deva pub
ere can be traced back to a deed of
312 stating that the owners were
Hugh de Brichull and his wife, Mary.
Hugh was a sheriff in 1286 and a mayor
from 1292 until 1313. He, or Robert de

Macclesfield, a later sheriff, built a house here.
In the 16th century a Tudor house was
built on the same site. By then the road
levels had risen: the foundation is a metre
above the old medieval drain. The Elizabethan
staircase still survives in the pub.

In the 17th century, the Moon Tavern was
the pub's name. Perhaps it is time to

'A mere passage'

St Peter's
Churchyard

follow in the footsteps of St Peter's
Church parishioners, who – after walking
the parish bounds in 1697 – adjourned
to the Moon Tavern.

Finish the route by descending the steps past St Peter's Church:

founded as St Peter's and St Paul's
on the present cathedral site, it was
rebuilt here when St Werburgh's relics
were brought to Chester. It appears
that only part of the dedication was
transferred, for in 1081 it was listed as
'Ecclesia Sancti Petri de Mercato'.

Inside is a rare brass figure: a memorial
to a Chester sheriff, Robert Townsend
who died in 1626.

At one time all pews haid to be paid
for, and there were regular disputes
in the cathedral's consistory court about
who had the pew when someone died.
Records of 1627 show 'Mr Richard Dutton
now Maior of this Sittie for half yeares
rent for his two pews iiijd' (4d).

NOW you have completed this tour
of 'Chester Inside Out', you may like
to sit on a pew for a rest and contemplate
that here, nearly two millenia ago,
was the *'principia'* or legionary HQ
for the Roman fortress of DEVA.

END OF WALK

STREET INDEX

NUMBERS refer to strip maps
(Streets in brackets are only on main map)